The POTTER and the CLAY

LYN CONSTABLE

Copyright: Lyn Constable

ALL RIGHTS RESERVED. This book is copyright protected. Apart from any fair dealings for the purpose of private study, criticism, research or review as permitted under the *Copyright Act (Australia)*, no part may be reproduced by any process without written permission. Enquiries should be addressed to the copyright owner.

 A copy of this book can be found in the National Library of Australia, Canberra

ISBN:: 978-1-7644921-1-9

Styling and formatting by Linda Ruth Brooks
Photographs: author's own
Memoir/autobiography/spiritual

Edited by Jill Dorey, Rachel Wherrett and Neridah Hoawerth on behalf of Hammond Care Champion Life.

'Oh Lyn, can I not do to you as this potter has done to his clay? As the clay is in the Potter's hand, so are you in My hand.'

Jeremiah 18:6 NLT

Contents

My Story 7
Eliza Redman 9
Uncovering the mystery of Eliza 10
My Parents 11
Growing up in Orange 21
Adolescence and Marriage 48
Motherhood and Family Life 50
Working Life and my Nursing Career 56
My Nursing Career Achievements 57
Leaving Orange 60
Working in Nursing Homes 62
Tough Times for our Family 68
Moving to Queensland 1998 76
    Sunshine Coast 76
    Blackall Western Queensland 79
Moving back to the Hunter Region 86
    Life in Cooranbong 92
A Journey I Never Thought I Would Have to Take 96
    Brett's Story 96
    Brett's Achievements in Education 97
    Brett's first major breakdown 1997 100
    Second major breakdown 2001 102
    Third major breakdown 2003 103
    Fourth Major breakdown 107

2010 - A Significant Year 124
    Retirement 2010 127
    My Life Changes Direction 129
    Volunteer Work 136
Guidance from God 137
Personal Interactions 138
    A Divine Appointment on Forgiveness 139
The Gift of Forgiveness - Connecting Matters 141
    How We Treat Others 142
Today 23 September 2024 144
Telling my Story 146
Until the Clouds Roll Back 149
    Brett's song 149

My Story

My name is Lynette Constable (née Walker), born in 1953 in Orange Base Hospital.

Me as a baby and as a toddler

I married Allan (Charlie) Constable (deceased). We had three children. I have eight grandchildren. I also have one great-granddaughter. The total treasures of my life.

My parents were Roy and Gladys Frances Walker (nee Ryan), they were married in Wellington, NSW on 1 September 1950, both deceased. They had six children.

I have five siblings, from the eldest to the youngest, Jazz (deceased 31/1/2017, at age 67), Jack, Tom (deceased 11/01/2020, at age 67), Julia and Maddy. I'm between Tom and Julia.

We grew up in Orange, Central West New South Wales. We were fortunate to have lived in a little street called Fox

Avenue which was bordered by Margaret Street and Matthews Avenue.

Twenty houses in all, full of young families and homes courtesy of the war service as the dads were war veterans. We kids in the street played together, fought together, and got up to mischief together, and in a way became extended family.

My mother was a stay-at-home Mum caring for six children. She was born in Girilambone on 4 December 1917. Mum died on 15 March 1996, at age 78. She was an only child to Charles Ryan (born in Mudgee, NSW) and Ada Winifred Ryan (née Ferguson) born 20/07/1892 in Nymagee and died 10/10/1972 in Bloomfield Hospital, Orange. They were married at St Tom's Church, Nyngan on 1 September 1917.

Mum's father left the family home when she was only three years old. The story goes that grandfather wanted a boy, not a girl, so he left. My grandmother never let my mother forget that and blamed my mother for her father's departure, which is where I believe Mum may have started her struggles with mental health.

Eliza Redman

I tell this story of Eliza Redman because she is the reason we are here. My great, great, great grandmother Eliza Redman nee Ferguson was born 11 May 1823, in London, England. She died 17 December 1898, at age 68 from old age and diarrhoea in Nyngan NSW.

Eliza's trade was known as a nurse and needlewoman. She was the beloved wife of John Dobbs Ferguson, died 20 March 1867 in Victoria. The mother of their children and grandchildren.

Uncovering the mystery of Eliza
(a clipping from the newspaper in Narromine)

Eliza was a courageous and talented young 16-year-old who was one of 180 convict women and 10 children transported on the ship RAJAH in 1841 from England to Hobart. Elisabeth Fry and her committee for prison reform, provided the women with material and sewing equipment, clothing, bibles, books and pencils as each convict went on board the ship.

During the long voyage at least 30 women worked on a quilt. Eliza is thought to be one of those women. The quilt was large and when completed a thank you note was embroidered on the bottom to Elisabeth Fry and her committee.

On arrival in Hobart the quilt was sent back to England to Mrs Fry. Four years later Mrs Fry died and the quilt was lost for 145 years. It was found in an attic in Scotland and returned to Australia in 1987.

The quilt is now in the National Gallery in Canberra known as the Rajah Quilt. It is a remarkable achievement of the convict women to create a thing of such beauty on the unstable deck of a nineteenth-century sailing ship. It is one of Australia's iconic textiles.

The full history can be found in the book, *Patchwork Prisoners: The Rajah Quilt and the Women Who Made It* by Trudy Cowley & DTomne Snowden

My Parents

My mother looked to her cousins for siblingship, they were all very tightly knitted together like family. They are all resting now till the resurrection morning.

My mother had two mental breakdowns in her younger life at ages 16 and 18 years. At 18 she was given shock treatment and deep sleep therapy. The doctors wanted Grandma to have her committed to the Mental Health Clinic but because of the treatment Mum received, Grandma said 'no, I will take her home and care for her myself'. Oh how awful that must have been for them both!

I realised later on in life that my mother suffered from a mental illness which greatly affected those around her. In my grandmother's old age, Mum had a shed built in the backyard in the late '50s and transformed it into a two-room flat by a neighbour called Mr Reg Scarr.

My grandmother lived there until she could no longer care for herself and was moved into a nursing home. Grandma was independent in taking care of her own bathing needs. She had an old timber commode chair with a potty for her toileting needs. Mum took her midday meals across to her. Grandma took care of her breakfast and dinner. While living with us, she came on our family outings including many picnics. We enjoyed having her around and loved her very much. What a pleasure it was to have her with us. I remember sitting at her feet as she read from her little black Bible. She read her Bible daily. Lovely times spent together for both Mum and Grandma. Until Christ's return when they will meet again.

Although Mum was an only child she had many aunts and uncles and heaps of cousins who were her extended family. She was very close to every one of them and richly blessed. We often wondered how and where Mum got the funds to do the upgrades to the house, new carpet, venetian blinds, furniture etc. My brother Jack replaced the old timber windows in the front of the house for her when they ceased to open. My sister Julia, when she started work, saved up and paid the last of the mortgage out, so Mum didn't have the worry of that hanging over her head.

There was an electrical shop, called Wiley's Electrical downtown where Mum would purchase items needed for the house and she would pay them off. One item I remember was our black and white Pye TV, the first in the street. Grandma won the deposit and Mum paid the rest in small payments till it was paid for. She would faithfully go downtown every week/fortnight and pay whatever amount she could afford. Mr Wiley would accept it graciously until he could say to her, 'Mrs Walker, your debt is paid.'

I guess she did the same for other items for the house as well. Sometimes we had the folk from the neighbourhood come and watch a program or two. Mr Kitt from across the road loved to come across every evening to watch the news but much to our (us kids') annoyance we were constantly told to shut up. We were raised with the 'children should be seen and not heard' thing.

Before we had a washing machine, Mum did the washing

by hand in double cement laundry tubs. There was an old hand wringer attached between the two tubs and she would go from tub to tub to get the washing and rinsing done until she got the old wringer machine, and then out on the line that strung across the yard attached to two post with crossbars to hang the clothes, best drying line ever! Attached to the side of one of those posts, Dad built a see-saw for us kids to play on! I remember that see-saw back in the '50s, maybe early '60s before the shed was built. Mum eventually replaced that old line with a Hills rotary clothesline.

Growing up in the '50s we didn't have a refrigerator, but we would have an ice chest and would have weekly deliveries of large blocks of ice to keep our food cold for the week.

Mum also volunteered later in her life as a Blue Lady at the Orange Base Hospital in the maternity unit folding nappies. She later became a Pink Lady and worked in the general wards where she would do shopping for those who didn't have any visitors or family.

She loved to crochet. She made many rugs, and we girls all got one of her rugs. She knitted squares for charities where they would be made up as blankets for families in need, some sent to the mission fields.

Mum loved Jesus and loved to spend time in His Word, listening to sermons on tapes as well as listening to gospel music. She was diligent in all that she did.

> 'To our mother, who saw us through good and bad times and gave all she had.'

My Father ... MyMother

My father was Roy Walker born in Gilgandra on 30 October 1917. Dad died 12 September 1992 in Orange, at age 74.

His father's name was Robert Alfred Walker, born 22 October 1891 at Macleay Street, Dubbo, his mother's name was Eliza Ann Methvin born at Baradine 1896, NSW. She was of Aboriginal origin from the Kamilaroi tribe, she died on 9 July 1934 at age 38 in Morisset Mental Health Hospital, Lake Macquarie NSW. Cause of death, dementia and chronic myocarditis.

She is buried in an unmarked grave at Morisset Cemetery. There is no record of her resting place as the Morisset Hospital at that time burnt down and all records were destroyed, therefore her gravesite could not be pinpointed as it is for many others buried there.

They had three sons, John, Roy (my Dad), and Ron.

When Grandma was pregnant with Ron my grandfather Robert died due to the black plague. John (aged 4) and Dad (aged 2) were taken from their Kamilaroi mother and placed in an orphanage. They were fostered out a few times, but when that didn't work out they were sent to a farm down near Goulburn where they attended various chores and duties as were given to them.

During that time, they were both regularly flogged by the farmhand. One day John stood up to the farmhand and made it clear that if he touched his brother again he would kill him.

After a while of fear, the boys ran away from the farm and hitchhiked down to Dandenong in Victoria where they found Aunty Jean, sister to Eliza Methvin, Dad's mother. The two boys stayed together for a time but were eventually separated.

Dad and John were from the stolen generation. In 1967/68 Dad was in Moss Vale working as a cook in a pub. One day as he looked out the window he saw a man working in the yard and realised it was his brother John. What a surprise that must have been! John and Dad were finally reunited again.

In later years my brother first met Uncle John in Moss Vale at the pub where they spent a bit of time together. John was in need of a new pair of shoes, so Jack offered to buy him a pair and John quite boldly said, 'Julius Marlow'.

Jack said, 'What!'

John said, 'I'll only wear Julius Marlow'.

It cost Jack $100! He said he'd never paid that much for a pair of shoes in his life. That must have thrilled Uncle John.

Meanwhile, my brother believes that when Grandma had baby Ron, he was moved around their Aboriginal families to protect him from being taken from his mother like his two brothers were. The loss my grandmother must have gone through must have been horrific for her.

Ron was fortunate enough to grow up with and around his family. I remember meeting Uncle Ron when I was young, he eventually ended up out at Coonabarabran where he lived out his life. Ron is buried in Coonabarabran along with other family members, including his son Wally who passed in 2023 and his brother John whom my brother had exhumed by the Aboriginal Council from an unmarked grave in the Field of Mars section of Rookwood Cemetery, Sydney. John was finally laid to rest next to his brother in Coonabarabran. How sweet that ending was. He was given a lovely memorial service and reburial by family members.

Dad and John had lost touch over the years but were about to get the surprise of their lives when they would finally meet again during WW2.

All three brothers were living in different parts of NSW when they enlisted in the 2nd World War. My father was 21 years old when he enlisted in the Australian Army.

It wasn't until the three brothers had signed up for service that they were able to find each other again in the Middle East where they would be reunited. Dad served in Turkey for six years. What an amazing reunion!

All three boys were able to return safely home! Both Dad and John came back from the war shell-shocked and suffered greatly as many others did. God loves families and loves to reunite them and unite them He did!

Before Dad left to go overseas he was working on a farm

where he had to do basic training. During Dad's time there, he encountered a tragedy which would change him for life. While driving a forklift he felt a bump under his wheel. He stopped and got out to see what it was, to his horror a small child (girl) was pinned under the wheel with her glazed eyes looking up at him. Dad never recovered from that tragedy.

My heart aches as I try to imagine what he must have gone through. Why that child was there at that time I do not know, maybe she lived in a nearby house on this farm and was watching with curiosity, who knows! Just tragic.

Amongst all the tragedy my father became an alcoholic which led to anger and abuse toward Mum. She always said that Dad wasn't the same man she married after the war, his whole personality had changed and he became physically abusive.

They loved each other even though their lives were buried under the rubble of their circumstances. They just couldn't live with each other. Before Dad died he spent time with Mum when she was in the hostel. He would go and pick her up and take her for a drive, like a date in old age!

When Mum went into the nursing home Dad would go and see her, he felt the pain of what he had done to her in their early years, he felt strong remorse for what he had done and blamed himself for her being in the nursing home. With tears in his eyes he said that she was the only woman that he ever truly loved. I think he died not long after.

The war had dealt harshly to all the men and women who gave their time and lives to serve and then had to come back to civilian life and live normally as if nothing happened and cope as best they could.

I remember when I was in primary school in the 6th grade and Dad was cooking at the Royal Hotel.

One day a couple of other girls and I left the school grounds and went to the hotel where my father was to see if he would make us some lunch, he told us to go back to the school and he would bring something to us. He came to the school a short while later with a big paper parcel of hot scallops and chips for us, what a feast! Another time when he was running a fish & chip shop over the east side of town, we kids would walk over there on a Sunday morning and help him with the peeling of the potatoes and then putting them in the potato cutter and turning them into chips. Good experience I say for us kids They were the best chips!

We didn't have a car. Our little feet were our transport. I remember when Dad was cooking at the Popular Cafe (it was the cafe to hang out at for all of us young guys and gals).

Dad got me a job there serving meals at the tables when I was 15. One day I took a tray to one of the tables with two meals on it, I sat one half of the tray on the table and picked up the plate that was on the table side of the tray and yes, you guessed it, leaving the other meal with no support on the outer side of the tray and yep, to the floor it fell!!

I can't remember if I picked the plate up off the floor and put it back on the tray or if I just ran with embarrassment back to the kitchen. My father and I had a fight over that and I walked out. He and I clashed often, maybe because we were so much alike. And that's all there is to say about that!

While working at the Caravilla Motel, which was on the

same side of town to the fish and chip shop, Dad would often make us breakfast. The only part I can really remember in my mind's eye is sitting at the table in the kitchen waiting for our brekky. Dad would also get us to roll the butter as well and there was a little gadget we used to make the curls. Also, there was a grassy slope out the front of the motel where we older kids would go out and lay on our sides and roll down the grassy slope, laughing, and then we would get back up and run up the slope to roll down again.

It was never hard for kids back then to make fun out of something so simple. Below is a lovely photo of all of us six kids with Dad sitting on the front lawn, with Spotty in the background. I love this photo. It shows me that Dad did spend quality time with his children.

All of us kids with Dad and Spotty

I tell these stories to remind me of good times with my dad. They played a big part in the struggles I certainly had as a young girl and the healing process in the "whys" of my girlhood and growing up with the void, at times, of a father in an abusive environment.

I missed him when he wasn't there. In the middle of the night when the house was in darkness I would cry wanting him to come home, why didn't he care about us kids, I would think? And whatever the reason it doesn't matter anymore. With time and God's healing power old wounds do heal.

Thinking back to the good times with Dad gives me happy thoughts and peace and how I would one day grow from the feeling of a rejected ugly duckling to a beautiful swan knowing forgiveness and restoration. God is good.

Growing up in Orange

When I started school at age five I decided I needed a haircut so I got Mum's scissors and cut my hair. I was sitting on the big bed in the girls' room and took the scissors to my hair. It didn't get me out of going to school nor did it get me out of family photos, I was also missing my front tooth! Not a good look to start kindy.

Julia and me with our bad haircuts

Despite what was happening around us, we kids always played together and laughed together. We had fun together. We would curl up around the radiogram listening to the funnies that were on the radio at that time. We played with our matchbox cars, and we carved out roads on the dirt driveway. We made roads and tunnels and built houses out of matchsticks and twigs, we had a lot of fun.

We had paddocks nearby that we played in. Up the road a bit and around the corner was a big vacant block where the plovers nested. We loved to jump the fence and wander across the paddock. As the plovers came swooping out of the grass we'd scream running and laughing jumping back over the fence, the plovers would then go back to their nests. And we would do it again.

There was a church over the back of our house situated in one corner of a big paddock where we'd go to Sunday school. I learnt about Jesus there and never forgot who He was even though I didn't understand anything about Him then. He has been my strength and comfort all my life and I didn't realise that when I was young until I grew and experienced His goodness.

There were rams and sheep in that same paddock, when they'd come down to the fence I'd climb up with a big stick and poke at the rams hard to rile them up. They would butt the fence with their horns, I would either nearly fall off or I would jump off. I look back now and think, 'how did I not break any bones!' and 'how did Mum put up with us kids, especially me?'

Mum used to say I was like six kids rolled into one and then she had five others to look after! I could never understand that. I wrecked the back fence because I decided to be cruel to the rams, they rammed their horns into the fence until it eventually warped and buckled and rocked like a reed in the wind.

I was always called a cow of a kid by my Aunty Norma,

she would tell me that she hoped I would have a kid just like me when I grew up. As I write this now, I can understand why. I would have killed the kid!

On the back fence we also had a chook pen where we kept some bantams, some chooks and later we had pigeons.

The side paling fence in the backyard is where I would climb barefoot, putting one foot on the top of the palings and the other foot on the side ledge so I could run the full length of that fence.

I remember over that side fence there was a gate connecting to our back neighbours the Gransdens, they had a stable just through that gate where they kept their horse. We had animals all around us. I must have driven my poor mother nuts. But the beauty of that paddock was the cherry trees! So we loved cherry picking too, in abundance!

Out in the back garden among the trees, we would erect our green canvas swimming pool where we loved to splash and play on those hot summer days. Near the pool was Hunt's yard, we kids used to climb the fence and eat the gooseberries from their bush that grew right on the fence.

We got into trouble for that too, . We did eventually get a swing set that consisted of a glider, monkey bars in the middle, and a single swing at the end. Many fun times on these swings. It was on the sidebar of the frame I remember that Dad cut our pet lamb Lucy's tail off when she was only weeks old, and we kids stood around and watched as the blood squirted out.

I also remember the ice cream man Mr Pearson or as he was called 'Mr Whippy.' I remember two or three large green canvas bags in the back of his truck filled with ice creams and ice blocks covered in dry ice. It was such a treat to run out with our threepence to buy an ice cream or ice block on a hot day.

And I remember the massive walnut tree we had in our backyard just right of our little pool. When they were ready they would drop to the ground underneath the tree and the ground would be covered with walnuts. Mum would fill all sorts of buckets and containers with walnuts and keep them in the laundry on the floor. We had walnuts galore which I think she would have shared with our neighbours.

We also had other trees, plums, and nectarines. They would eventually be removed to make way for the shed. Mum was a keen gardener, she grew lots of things from cuttings. We didn't have a lot of money, but Mum would grow our own fresh fruit and vegetables that we never went without. God's watchful eye and His provision for our needs were always present.

I remember the outhouse we had in the backyard in the '50s before the sewer went on, where we had a sewer man (as we called him) come every week to change all the pans in the street.

One day the man arrived to change the pans over in our yard. As he picked up the full pan and swung it up onto his shoulders (as they did), the bottom fell out of the pan. I will leave the story there and you can use your own imagination on what that poor man must have experienced. I can't even imagine the clean-up, and the look on Mum's face, not to mention the poor man - this was a house of eight people!

And we evil little humans probably laughed our heads off.

Another thing I remember is Mum running the bath for five of us kids, we bathed together when we were little. We jumped in the tub having our usual splash and laugh together when all of a sudden someone yelled, 'What's that!' (you could play the Jaws music here).

Tom had pooped in the bath and there it was, a big brown log floating on top of the water. We all jumped up screaming and yelling, 'Muuuum, Tom pooed in the bath!'

We scampered out of the tub falling over each other, water going everywhere. Tom is still sitting there in the water laughing. I don't remember him getting out in a hurry. It was funny

We enjoyed Christmases, we had the live tree up to the ceiling. Balloons hanging on the branches, we had streamers we made ourselves, pinned from corner to corner of the ceiling, and around the tree. Then hanging all the other decorations with them. And gifts we would find under the tree on Christmas morning. I remember us having a white Christmas three times when we were kids.

It was never a surprise to us to get four seasons in one day growing up in Orange, having snow in the summer was no surprise!

Over in the paddocks near where we lived, the boys would make holes in the ground and cover them with grass so the holes couldn't be seen. Then they would crawl into the blackberry bushes where they had carved out tunnels and hide, so that when the boys who lived up the hill in Phillip St came down to fight, they would fall in the holes. They could never find the boys hidden away in the blackberry bushes! . It amazes us when we talk of it today that no one got hurt or broke any bones or got bitten by snakes! What a treat those old days were!

In those same paddocks, we'd roll on the grass to flatten it and make hallways and rooms. It was like a big cubby house surrounded by blackberry bushes and tall pine trees, the grass was chest-high and dry as a chip in the summertime. As children, we were lucky to have the freedom to have these paddocks as our playground, not just us but all our friends and surrounding neighbours too.

Our parents knew each other, and some became good friends and all of us kids played together. We were like an extended family. Not just the kids from our street but from the surrounding streets as well. We played at night under the streetlights until it was time to come in when our mums called us.

Some of the boys would get some tin cans and tie long strings to them and then sit them on the front verandas of the houses and hide behind the bushes and pull the string until the can came crashing down making a loud racket. The parents in the houses would come out and yell 'get out of here, I know who you are!' at the boys for their shenanigans. It was fun. Or we could join tin cans together with an extra long piece of string and make walkie-talkies, just put the can up to your ear while the other person talked into the can at the other and you could hear them, it worked a treat.

We'd wander off on weekends, school holidays, and walk the hills to go mushrooming, asking Mum's permission of course. We had our pails with us to put the mushrooms in. We climbed the tall pine trees just over the back of the houses across the street from us and we would see who could get to the top first. We would go blackberry picking as well, and Mum would make jam.

The schoolyard was like a big paddock with timber school buildings up near the fence close to the road on Margaret Street. There was a great big fig tree there that produced amazing figs. Those figs! Oh, how I remember standing under that tree and just eating them. And they were so big! They were the real deal, not the tiny little things you get at the supermarket nowadays that have no flavour to them. These were sweet and not pale pink, they were almost red. They were maroon, deep pink. So we had figs, cherries and blackberries, bliss!

Bletchington Public School was just up the end of Fox Ave connecting to Matthews Ave, the school went up to second grade. It was here where I kissed a boy, he had long blond curly hair and was so cute! From memory, I think his name was Michael. I chased him down that paddock, tackled him, and then kissed him! I would have been six or seven. I don't know what got into me. I have often wondered if he remembers that day and shudders.

There was a family out on Canobolas Road, the Williams, who had an orchard where we went and picked pears. I remember one time when Mum was very sick with pneumonia and had to go to the hospital, we kids were fostered out to various places to be cared for, as Dad was often away. One of those homes belonged to the minister of the Methodist church in Anson St where Jack and Jazz went, and Tom went to the Gransdens' home around the corner. Julia was placed in the Costello's home across the street up on the corner.

I went to my grandmother's house about a mile away, Dad would put me on his pushbike and off we'd go. When we were almost there outside Mackie's Store on the corner of Dalton and McLachlan Street, I managed to stick my foot in the spokes and down we would both go into the gutter. How I loved to stay with Grandma! I remember the puffed wheat with hot milk and the thick cream like a blanket over the top. There was a big galvanised bathtub that I would have a bath in and Grandma's feather bed after to sleep in. It was always a treat to stay with Grandma!

Another time Mum was in hospital having Maddy and we were placed again with the neighbours, only this time I went to the Eyles house just across the street.

Mrs Eyles used to check her kids' bums for worms, I remember one of the girls saying, 'Check Lynette if she's got worms' I was mortified! Luckily that didn't happen! Things people do behind closed doors. Julia went to Costello's house, and Tom again to Gransdens'. I'm not sure where Jack and Jazz went that time.

I see the love and care shown in our little street. It was family-oriented, with everyone looking out for each other (even the worms).

Another time I remember Mum and Dad taking us up to Mt Canobolas, we hopped in the backseat of Dad's 1950 Armstrong Siddeley dual cab ute, grey in colour with a blue stripe up the side, which I might add, Dad gave Jazz and Jack paint brushes to help him paint the car this colour. And no seat belts in those days. You can imagine what it must have looked like with five of us cramped in the little back seat and Maddy sitting on Mum's lap in the front seat.

We would have a lovely day out up the mountain, coming back down the mountain though was always a bit scary as it was a windy gravel road with a lot of potholes and ditches, it was a rough ride. As we drove through the town heading home, we may have stopped to have ice cream, I'd like to think we did. As we came closer to home about four blocks away, our trip became a hairy ride when the brakes failed on Dad's dual cab ute just before the intersection of Dalton Street and Lord's Place.

Dad quickly turned the corner into Dalton Street to prevent an accident and ran into the gutter to stop the truck. We all climbed out, I guess a little shaken, but no one was hurt. We weren't far from home so we may have walked home with an exciting story to tell the kids in our street and take to school the following week. Life wasn't always dull.

In my teens, I got a job on an orchard on Philip Street just over the back of the school picking pears. It was a heavy job but I didn't mind. I learnt to drive the tractor, a little old grey Massey Ferguson. That was probably my very first job before the job at Myers. It was fun!

Every Sunday we four older kids used to walk to the pool barefoot. One of us would usually trip and kick our big toe, causing it to bleed and the top nearly peel off. It was a different kid each week but always the big toe. We would laugh about it, it was so funny, except for the one who kicked their toe that week of course!

Another funny thing I remember about our family is that at mealtimes, we had a long table in the kitchen with two long bench stools on either side where we would sit, three on each side. If we wanted to talk, we would stand up (and that wasn't an easy task to do, clambering over the bench), have our say and then climb back over the bench and sit down. Then, the next one would stand up and say something as if 'Hey, I've got something to say!'

I look back at that now and think how odd and funny that was, I'd like to think how unique we were as kids in our ways as a family. I guess we felt we had something important to say worthy of standing up to speak, and in our unique way, you can see that in the adults we became.

An embarrassing but funny memory was when Mum had us older ones wash up after dinner. She had these copper-coloured steel pads to scrub the pans that reminded us kids of the lady next door's hair as she was a curly headed redhead. We would fight over the steel pad yelling 'I wanna use Mrs Hunt's hair.' We were evil little human beings! Mum was beside herself flapping her hands telling us to keep quiet as Mrs Hunt might hear us.

Another time in the kitchen it was my turn to wash the dishes, so I tried to get out of it by saying, 'I need to go to the toilet!' and off I went and stayed there for a bit then came out thinking all would be finished, only to find, surprise, surprise the dishes were waiting for me. You cannot pull the rug over your mother's eyes! Fact.

A black Vanguard was sitting in the backyard that belonged to Tom where at one time he kept a small black pig. So of course, I would regularly go and stick my head in the window and stir it up.

One day I opened the door, and it got out and we were all running around the yard chasing this pig, kids screaming trying to catch it and put it back in the car. Oh dear, the things we used to do! I remember capturing a spider, I think it was a huntsman. I put it in a glass jar, filled it up with water and watched it squirm (I never did that again it was just that once). I still hate spiders today, and I do kill them! Sorry.

Lucy, our pet lamb, ate a bit of Mum's cactus that was sitting on the front veranda, and she was poisoned. We found her the next morning dead in her pen. We loved her so much! She was the only pet we buried in the backyard, we put wire over the top to keep any critters from digging at it and we put a white cross with 'Lucy' written on it.

Maddy and I with our 'pet' magpie Jackie

We had a lot of pets: a pet magpie we called Jackie. He used to come to the backdoor every Sunday morning tapping with his beak on the door wanting his breakfast, we could hand feed him. We had a pet possum that lived in the laundry, where the toilet was as well. The possum would sit up on the cement cistern high above the toilet and you had to pull the long chain that was connected to the mechanism to release the water to flush the toilet.

One day we found our possum gone and figured he must have fallen into the toilet and someone pulled the chain and flushed him, we never saw him again. We also had rosellas and a galah (he belonged to Grandma). Mum bred rosellas, she'd have the featherless babies wrapped in blankets on the living room table and would feed them porridge from a spoon. We also had cats but the only dog I remember was our beloved Spotty.

Spotty Spotted: Spotty made the headlines in the *Dubbo Liberal Edition*. Dad had taken Spotty with him to Dubbo and while there his car broke down and had to be taken to the garage to be fixed.

During that time Spotty became lost, it was 23 March, early '60s. Spotty was our trusted friend and guardian for eight years. Dad had made a fruitless search for Spotty and returned home without him. I do remember how upset we kids were when Spotty got lost.

Sometime after the event, Spotty was noticed in West Dubbo by Ann (13) of O'Donnell Street as she recognised him from his photo in the *Liberal*, she managed to catch him and her mother rang the newspaper. A telegraph was sent to our Aunty Norma and she went out to Dubbo to pick Spotty up and bring him home to us kids who missed him so much. Spotty lived on to be an elderly dog and was put down due to cancer.

I have treasured memories of our family picnicking at Ophir. Ophir was a beautiful area from the gold mining days. I remember the winding dirt road that took you down to the creek. There was an old cement bridge that went across the creek that took you to the picnic spot where we could put our swimmers on, go in the creek and walk over the rocks. There were caves as well that we loved to explore although I didn't like to go too far into the caves as I was scared of the dark.

We had the most beautiful scrub picnic in the summertime under the shade of a tree. We were so well set up, picnic rugs, baskets and boxes, thermoses, a cake tin and other bits and pieces they brought with them. Mrs Quinlan and Miss Norkway were good friends of our family.

Mum, Mrs Quinlan and Miss Norkway would lay the food out on the blanket, and we would all sit around the outside. Mrs Quinlan lived down the bottom of Fox Avenue and Miss Norkway lived in Hill Street which was about four blocks from our place. They made shorts and long pants for the boys out of old men's trousers and our girl's dresses were made from second-hand women's skirts. Mum would sit up late at night sewing, it was also the time she got all the housework done, she did like a clean house.

Mum would have been lost without these two ladies. They were amazing people and loyal friends, they were like family. We often visited their homes. There was always a treat of biscuits or cake on our visits.

Our mother always saw to it that we had plenty of fresh air and sunshine and family togetherness.

Uncle Walter was Mum's uncle, grandma's brother and he took a lot of the photos of us kids when we were growing up. He would bring his piano button accordion to our place and a big tape recorder. He taped us kids when we least expected it then he would play the tapes back to us and we would laugh.

When Mum's aunts and cousins would visit, they would be in the kitchen either preparing food or cleaning up, we would hear a lot of chatting and laughter. Uncle Walter would set the recorder up near the kitchen door and tape them. When they were finished cleaning up or cooking, he would play the recording back and they would go crook at him and then have a good laugh. He also would bring slides and his projector and we would have our slide night of all the photos he had taken over the years. What a treat, it was so wonderful. Our own movie show without leaving the house. It was wonderful light fun and such a treat to have these precious souls staying with us.

We would sit around the fire, and Uncle Walter would always have a yarn to tell. He would get out his harmonica and play a tune or play his button accordion. Jazz would play her recorder; I remember her playing *Twinkle Twinkle Little Star*. He was just the best uncle; he was witty and funny and a joy to have around. He was a bachelor and lived out west in Girilambone with his sisters. He lived in a small shed just behind his sister, Aunty Mealie's house.

I remember it being cluttered with heaps of treasures with his bed in one corner. It would have been a treasure trove of memories of photos and slides of us kids that we lost after he died. Family members of Uncle Walter that we didn't know got all his things. He would have had enough info to mark out our family tree.

Uncle Walter would drive to visit us every year in his 1956 grey FC Holden station wagon and would stay with us overnight. He would then drive to Lithgow, leave his car, and catch the train to the Sydney Show. He always stayed at the People's Palace while in Sydney. He would stay for the duration of the show and then he would catch the train back to Lithgow, get his car, travel back to our place, and stay a while before heading back to Giri. He later traded that car in for a yellow Torana.

The show is where he would update his cameras and recorders as well, I remember the first black and white Instamatic camera he bought. He came back from the show and took photos of us kids, he had to put the photo under his arm and hold it there for a bit for it to develop in the warmth of his armpit and then paint a clear coating on it and let it dry to seal it. He later traded it for the YouBute model where it developed itself and was colour! He loved new inventions, he was a man of gadgets. It was such a treat to have him around.

I remember the milk cart, pulled by two draft horses. It would often be early in the morning, with these beautiful draft horses with the steam coming out of their nostrils, and you would hear the tinkle of the milk bottles being dropped off on the veranda. Our baker was a man named Kevin Thomas (who later married Aunty Norma), he was a good worker and was always on the move. He drove a van and had a big monstrous basket which he would pack with bread with a cover over it, he would flip back the cover and deliver fresh bread to each house on the street.

We had a lot of family members from out west that came to stay with us like Uncle Walter and his sisters and brothers, Auntie Mealie, Auntie Myrtle, Auntie Jess, Auntie Mavis, Bub & Jack, and Uncle Sam & Aunty Edna and Aunty Jean, Aunty Pat to name a few and all the cousins that came with them. We had great support from our extended family and a lot of fun, we loved these relatives so much. They would come down from Girilambone and Dubbo.

We spent a lot of holiday time out at Girilambone as well. I have a lot of family snapshots in Geri with the red dirt up the walls of the houses, the cars covered in red dirt.

Riding our bikes, playing under the hose in our swimmers, just having simple country fun. We would have races to see how far we could run across the hot red dirt barefoot, it was so hot you could fry an egg on it! We had such wonderful times full of fun and laughter unless you got stung by a large wasp, ouch!

Aunty Mellie had her shower out the back of her house and the wasps would have their nests around it, so it was always touch-and-go not to be stung.

When Aunty Jess would come to visit, especially in the winter, she loved to put her chair right in front of the fire along with Mum and whoever else. She was very wide in the rear and would take up all the view of the flames of the fire. Us kids had to sit on the floor behind her, we were mortified, no heat from the fire! We loved her just the same as all the others, but!

I have lovely photos of the family in the park having picnics; Grandma, Mum and Dad with his ANZAC medals, and us kids all dressed in our finest. ANZAC Day started with the commemorative services held at the war memorial at dawn in Robertson Park. The ceremony: an introduction, hymn, prayer, an address, laying of wreaths, a recitation, the *Last Post*, a period of silence, the *Rouse* or *Reveille*: the bugle call, and the national anthem.

This all happened in Robertson Park. Later in the day, current and former servicemen and women would meet to take part in the marches. All of Orange would come out to enjoy this commemorative day. Both sides of the main street would be packed with people. What a treat!

At 15 I left school because Mum couldn't afford the fees. I had just started year nine and was making better grades.

My first job was at Myers, I was there for maybe eight or nine months and for some reason left and then went on the dole. I paid board whilst at Myers but when on the dole I stopped, maybe because of a drop in wages that went from $16 a week to $4 a fortnight!

When I didn't give Mum money from the dole she called the welfare to come and visit, and they took me aside to talk to me about this.

They told me if I didn't give Mum any money they would

take me away and put me in a home. I felt fear after being spoken to by the authorities, that if I didn't do as I was told I would go into foster care. To this day I have very little trust in welfare and the mental health system.

I discovered that Mum put a lock on her bedroom door and locked food in her room so I couldn't 'steal' any, I was so mad. I had a small cupboard in my room next to my bed that I would buy food and keep in there so I would have something to eat if I had nothing else.

The only thing I remember is the things that needed to be in the fridge, which I still had access to. I did my own washing so the laundry powder was still in the laundry. I did not understand why this happened and became frustrated and angry. It was a time when things were difficult. As I write these stories now I see God's mercy and grace through the brokenness of our precious family!

From that experience, I always had a fear of being locked away and maybe even going without, I would have nothing to do with welfare when I grew up. I felt they weren't to be trusted. I had a strong need to stay in control of my emotional self.

I was always a very strong-willed child and that rolled into my adulthood. I stood firm in what I believed and my stubbornness at times has been my worst enemy.

Today I don't see the angry emotional girl/woman I once was. I have forgiven those you have hurt me and I have been forgiven for those I have hurt. I now have peace in my heart and am more content than I have ever been. I found a quote that sums it up: 'Sometimes God takes you on a journey you didn't know you needed, to bring you everything you ever wanted. Trust the plan.'

In the early years of childhood, my home seemed to be good even though it was filled with physical, mental and emotional abuse leading to a lot of trauma in my life.

There were many happy snapshots of memories but in the early years, I remember feeling like I never belonged. I felt different. Always told I was useless or a cow of a kid, good for nothing. I used to tell myself that I was an only child and that this was a family that I unfortunately had to grow up with (and that's an awful thing to think), but that's how empty the space was around me at that time.

I remember the horrible abuse and ridicule, it wasn't constant, but it was there. Often it could be something as small as taking food from the fridge, making something and getting it wrong which would result in me curled in the corner of the cupboards beaten as my punishment.

I recall one time in my teens when my mother was belting me, and I got so mad that I raised my hand and slapped her across her shoulder (I have since asked God to forgive me for that). I told her I had had enough and to never hit me again, and I went to my room.

The next thing I remember Tom coming down the hall into my bedroom, pulling me off my bed by the hair, dragging me into the hall and smashing my head into the floor. This happened several times. Another time was in the kitchen. I often thought I would never make it to 15 (let alone past it).

My mother was a Christian, she went to church every

week, read her bible and prayed daily. I couldn't for many years understand how abuse and God came together. It's a miracle that I survived as long as I have with no brain damage, no dementia.

I remember in 2018 I woke in the middle of the night. I was pondering over my past with God and thought about all this and wondered how I survived as I did. It came to my mind that the only way I could have survived was that God had cupped my head in the palm of His hands protecting my brain, so I sobbed and praised Him for His love and protection.

I was told by my sister 30 years later that the abuse from my brother was instigated by my mother. Mum would pace the front path waiting for Tom to walk up the road and when she saw him, would run down to meet him saying something to him that only God knows, and he would come home in a rage. I've never been able to fathom this. I don't think about it now; it is in God's hands not mine.

Looking back, I realise just how much we were subject to, the terrible abuse from our father towards our mother and my mother toward me.

I remember as a young girl jumping on Dad's back at times to try and stop him from hurting Mum, she had blood on her face and clothes, leading up to bruising on her face. My two younger sisters would be huddled on either side of her crying. I wondered where my brothers were, and why they weren't helping me.

I learnt years later that they were in the kitchen laughing and I cried, I couldn't understand why they didn't try and protect Mum as well. In counselling sessions, I had years later, I discovered that it was out of fear of the scene before them, it was either laugh or cry. They were certainly tough times.

Oh how I felt the pain of rejection, of feeling unloved, not wanted, of not feeling safe in my home, they were horrid times and yet it amazes me how many fond memories of childhood we were given, threading their way through and overshadowing the memories of those bad times, and how these experiences and trials have shaped who I am today.

1 Peter 1:7 tells us; 'These trials will show that your faith is genuine'. My faith in God has always been strong and much stronger today. I must say, the good memories certainly outweigh the bad.

Despite this, I never hated God, never disbelieved in Him, I just believed that He hated me. It took me many years of searching for answers, I needed answers!

I was 40 when I started my journey of healing by having counselling sessions. I remember being given a tape by Louise Hay called *Loving the Child Within*. I would play that in my car driving to work and returning home, and I would cry all the way to and from work every day.

I couldn't perform this task straight away, it was so hard. It took a while, then one day I just decided to do it, I knew I needed this to heal from the brokenness within me and the journey begins. In my mind's eye I went to that child crying in the corner and I picked her up and held her in my arms, told her I loved her and that she was okay, and I sobbed. I had to keep doing that for a while. I hated the child within so much growing up, but that day was the beginning of a love relationship between me, the adult and the child within. It certainly didn't happen overnight, but it did happen! It was a long journey.

I then found a book on *The Strong-Willed Child* by Dr James Dobson. I couldn't put it down, I cried and I laughed, it was here that I discovered that I was not useless or good for nothing in any sense of the word, but a 'strong-willed child!' Seriously, I thought, is that all I was? What a relief that was to me. It was an amazing discovery! I continued to grow. I was then given another book to read by a dear friend of mine Linda, called *ADD in Adults* by Dr Gordon Serfontein, a wonderful book!

I found the pieces of the puzzle that were missing within me. I felt like a piece of Swiss cheese, full of holes and emptiness that needed to be a full block of solid cheese but still soft. The softness didn't come for a long time. I remained hard for many years. That hardness still raises its ugly head at times, but I'm softer than I used to be. I'm a work in progress and God's timing is perfect.

All of the brokenness, twisted love, fear, uncertainty, betrayal, selfishness, and rejection all mingled together, it was only through forgiveness that I would eventually find restoration that only God could give. The good times, the precious moments are more prominent in my mind now than the bad times. It's like my eyes are dimmed to the bad and are now veiled that I no longer see darkness and pain.

My relationship with my brother Tom was always good. My Mum was my Mum, and I loved her for that. My children were her grandchildren, I didn't take them from her, I visited always at her home (and later in the hostel then nursing home). I took her shopping, she babysat for me when I worked. I still involved her in my life. I would take her to visit Maddy or Tom when I could. When I went back to church at 21 my involvement with her was good, picnic lunches in the park, we did meals-on-wheels together.

We enjoyed church socials and outings together. Mum and I attended a Friendly Family Bible Program together, organised by the Seventh Day Adventist Church in Blayney on 3 December 1967, when I was 13. We both received a lovely black Bible for attending every night. I still have that Bible and now Mum's as well. We also attended the SDA annual Big Camp Meetings in Coulbourn in the '70s when my kids were young. They ran for a week and we would share a tent with my two younger sisters Julia, and Maddy. The best fun, and the best friendships and the best camps one could ever attend. Mum and I had wonderful times together, we laughed and we loved. The Bible says, 'God restores what the locusts destroyed.' I believe that!

Although life at home was difficult for us, we handled it in our own ways. Being children, we didn't talk about it with each other, we just coped as best we could. Julia and I talk about our family history quite a bit now and she said to me 'you've got no idea how it affected me.'

It's good to spend time together now and be open and honest with each other. My brother Jack and I do the same as well. My younger sister Maddy and I have always been close and have always been open to talking about past stuff. God has always been good to our family. He understood our brokenness and has led us into a closer relationship with each other as we got older. For that I'm grateful.

Jack went with Dad to the shearing sheds, on 26 March 1967 when he was 14. Mum was devastated. Somewhere along the way, Jack ended up in Bathurst with Jazz. Tom spent more time with families that had a lot of love and peace around them where Tom would feel the love and security he needed. He threw himself into boxing (became state champion at 14) and football (had a top reputation of being very good). Jazz left home at 15 with her boyfriend Jock and lived in Bathurst with his family until they got married. A lot of hurt threaded amongst those stories.

There is a quote that says, '*God has a thousand ways in which we know nothing of, to provide for our needs.*' God provided for all our needs as children and still continues to provide for us today in a way of which we know nothing. To me, that's the goodness of God.

Years later my brother Jack was telling me about his first visit to Coonabarabran and how he felt a strong connection in that place and how he felt at home. I said I felt the same when I visited for a weekend church camp. Friends of mine from Newcastle had bought some land and moved to Coonabarabran, and a couple of years ago they organised a church camp and we all went out for the weekend.

While I was there I had a strong feeling of connection to Coonabarabran. I told one of the ladies from the local church that I was of Aboriginal origin on my father's mother's side and that most of his family lived here. Often when Dad went walk-a-bout it was Coonabarabran he went to, to be with his family and yet we never knew anything about them, he never spoke of them. There are a lot of Walkers living in the area and many are buried in the Aboriginal cemetery.

As I was telling one of the ladies the story and how 'I felt a strong connection, that I felt a belonging here'. I didn't want to go home, I wanted to stay. Jack said he felt the same way. The fact of knowing that Coonabarabran is filled with the history of our Aboriginal heritage, our father's family is why we both felt that same strong connection.

Our Dad left the family home on 6 June 1966, I was 13. He moved around a lot. In his younger days he cooked in the shearing sheds and later in life, hotels in various places. In his later years in Orange, he worked in various hotels until he retired. Dad stayed in Orange until his death.

In late August 1992, Dad had begun having headaches and Maddy took him to the hospital where he stayed the night. She picked him up the next morning and took him to the doctor. Dad told the doctor that he had been having bad headaches which he said he had never suffered from in his life. The doctor said he was getting old and told him that he needed to be in a nursing home to which he replied, 'I will die first before I go to a nursing home.'

Dad was living with Jack, but at this time Jack was away, so Maddy took him back to her place. He went to lie on the bed for a while as he was feeling very tired. Maddy prepared tea for the family and told the boys to go and wake Grandad up as tea was ready. The boys found him on the floor and ran to get their mum. Maddy called an ambulance. They said it looked like he had had a stroke. While he was in the ambulance, he had several heart attacks and then more when he got to casualty and again in ICU.

When we were notified, that Dad had suffered a stroke, Julia and I drove down to Orange. I remember when I walked into Dad's room at the hospital and saw him lying there, I just stood at the foot of his bed and looked at him and he turned his head slightly and looked at me with tears in his eyes. I had tears in my eyes, and knew in my heart that all had been forgiven (my heart was breaking).

I knew that there was finally peace and there was nothing bad between us. I went beside him and wiped the drool from his mouth and gave him a drink on a swab as he couldn't swallow very well, and he just looked at me. He passed away two weeks later on 12 September 1992.

Dad was given a graveside funeral which was very nice. As I was walking to the grave site, I remember turning and looking to the left and saw the mound of dirt where the grave had been dug then to the right, I saw his coffin in the hearse. The reality of what was happening hit me, I broke down and sobbed. My brother Tom came to me, held me and comforted me. Again, in spite of the bad times, we chose love over evil and to give rather than take. Dad was given a beautiful send-off with the *Last Post* and the bugle call. Very emotional.

After hearing the stories of my parents' backgrounds, I can now honestly say it wasn't hard to forgive them both.

They were broken people, torn from family, rejected and battered. They were victims of victims as we were. Forgiveness heals. Forgiveness frees you to move forward and see life through new lenses. I learnt that in my own brokenness later in my life.

In 1983 Maddy and I were packing up Mum's unit as she was moving into full-time care. As Maddy and I were doing all the cleaning, Tom turned up and Maddy started to shake. He and I were just chatting about general stuff and what had to be done.

After Tom left I looked at Maddy and she was trembling. I said 'What's the matter? I hadn't realised how much Maddy was affected by his abuse of me. I didn't realise how deep the scars were in my own siblings! I told her that it was ok to let it go, that I had forgiven Tom and that I never held that against him. We were both victims of a victim. Maddy could be with each of us on our own, but when we came together she became frightened. Today Maddy has very little memory of those bad times, only the bruising on Mum's face. She has chosen to shut them out and that is okay.

When my brother Tom died suddenly in January 2020, my heart broke. I sobbed when they lowered him into the ground and my nephew Nathan, Maddy's youngest son, put his arm around me and comforted me. Death can feel cold and empty from pain and grief, yet it can still be filled with love, laughter and togetherness.

This was the same month and year that my Brett had had his fourth major breakdown.

Adolescence and Marriage

I went to Orange High School. I wasn't the best academically. I always had low grades until I reached my ninth year and moved up to a better level. Unfortunately, it was then that I had to leave school due to Mum's financial status.

I had several good friends. I had my first boyfriend there and my first kiss when I was 14 (second if you count the boy I tackled and kissed when I was six), we all had fun. My brother Tom was there, then my sister Julia came along just before I left, and then Maddy started high school after.

Two of my best friends were Rosalie and Meredith. Rosalie and I grew up in Fox Avenue, across the road from each other. We played together at age four before starting kindy together and went to the same primary school, not always in the same class but certainly in the playground. Meredith joined us in primary school, we became inseparable. We hung out a lot together, chasing boys was one adventure.

Meredith's parents owned Robert's Photography and Mr Roberts' brother owned Robert's Bakery. Cream buns and custard slices were to die for, and their meat pies were yummy! We hung out in both places many times. We hung out in the phone booth not far from my home where we had many boy/girl chats. I don't know how, but one call we made to one boy in town also connected us to another boy out of town who were both friends, so it ended up a three-way conversation, it was the funniest thing, When we grew up of course life changed and we three moved on in different directions.

Many years later I was visiting Orange, and walking through the main shopping centre, and the next thing Rosalie and her husband Ray came along! We hugged and sat down and had a wonderful time chatting. I said to Rosalie, wouldn't it be funny if Meredith passed by. You would not believe it, yes, there was Meredith!! I screamed with excitement! and called out to her and we three sat for ages chatting. We hadn't seen each other in many years, if not school! What a reunion!

When I first met my husband Charlie, he was 17 and I was 15. He was a spray painter, he was apparently very good, the best in town I believe. His place of work was down Post Office Lane at the back of Myers. When he left there he went to work as a mechanic at Wal McGarity car repairs.

I got pregnant at 17 to get away from home. Charlie's mother wanted me to be placed into the care of the Salvation Army to have my baby and have it adopted out, but Mum refused. I didn't know this at the time, Mum told me years later. Charlie and I were married on 23 October 1971. Mum arranged my wedding. She got a pastor from her church to marry us in her home. It was a small family gathering. My father did the catering.

Motherhood and Family Life

I had my first baby at 18. Jeff, born January 1972, 7lb 2oz Brett born June 1973, 5lb 6oz and Sarah born September 1977, 7lb 12oz. By 23 I had my family.

Although Charlie and I got along very well most of the time, it was a rocky marriage at different times. We stayed together for 16–17 years. We'd been boyfriend/girlfriend for two years prior to getting married. I spent a lot of time around his family. In our married time we lived in four different houses in Orange.

When we married we first lived with Charlie's mum for a bit. She and I had a bit of a fallout. I had chosen to attend prenatal classes and she thought if I helped her with housework I wouldn't need prenatal classes, so we had a spat over that. I also loved to go rabbiting with the boys. I was eight months pregnant at the time, it was fun up hill down dale and over the fences. I had a very active and healthy pregnancy, what could possibly be the problem?

I got a bee in my bonnet, dug my heels in and moved out, that's the stubbornness coming out. I found a one-bedroom flat above some shops on the corner of Summer and Peisley Streets next to the railway line.

There were 22 stairs to climb to reach the top, great exercise! My brother Tom helped me with part of the bond, it was $16 a week rent. Charlie decided to come with me and we moved to our new abode.

Charlie's Mum worried about me after I had Jeff. She would say, if I needed any help with bathing, or feeding the bub she was willing to help. I said, nope, I'm quite capable of doing things on my own, mmm.

We had a little 850-mini to get around in. We became very good friends with an older couple in the corner flat, Betty and Goog Sharp, he owned a barber shop. Charlie was earning $35 a week at the time when his boss gave him a raise of $10, which was certainly a bonus to now have $45.

It was here that I went into labour and had Jeff in the Orange Base Hospital Maternity Unit on 30 January 1972, he was adorable! His cry was louder than the other babies and he'd wake all the other babies up, especially when it came to the next feed. He was a good healthy baby. I learnt to knit here and knitted Jeff two jumpers.

I did suffer postnatal depression after having him and had to take anti depression medication for a while.

Charlie and I put our names down for a housing commission home while there. I fell pregnant with Brett here as well. During my first five months of pregnancy I was very sick and had two threatened miscarriages only six weeks apart. Both times I had to have total bed rest with a week in the hospital each time.

Before Brett was born, Housing came through and we moved to Casey Crescent into a two-bedroom commission home. Brett was born on 3 June 1973, in the same maternity unit where I had Jeff. He was a tiny little redhead and so cute. He was a very unwell baby. I didn't see him for the first 15 hours after his birth. He had trouble feeding and had to be tube fed. My mother-in-law didn't think he would survive. Brett didn't pick up until he reached five months.

He then went full steam ahead. He was such a solid stocky little boy. I didn't get my licence until I was 23, so I did a lot of walking when I had the boys.

L-R Brett, me and Jeff at Orange Pool

Casey Crescent was a good place to live. I made friends with the lady next door and Barbara the lady across the street. We made friends with a pommy couple, Bob & Chris and their two girls. We had some of the best times with this couple until they decided to go back to England where their families were. It was here I felt an emptiness and was impressed to go back to church to give my boys a solid belief in God, for me to be fed spiritually and feel secure in my own life. I was re-baptized here in 1975. I stayed in the church for 13 years before leaving again due to marital issues.

I have fond memories of living in Casey Crescent. We lived here for two years before we were offered a brand new three-bedroom commission house on the other side of town in Amaroo Crescent, where our daughter Jayne was born.

We lived at Amaroo Crescent for 10 years. A lot of good times were had there. We did have many holidays up at my sister Julia's place with her family in the Newcastle area.

It was here that I started a house cleaning job with a couple of good friends, Wendy and Sue. We had many clients and I worked three days a week. We went in pairs unless it was a big job that required the three of us. We did this for three years and had some great times. We continued our friendship and often got together. We remain friends although we don't see each other. Sue lives in Orange, I live in the Hunter and Wendy lives in Port Stevens. Great memories!

The fourth house was the one we bought together in Frost St, it was my favourite house, I thought we'd be there till death do us part. We were there for four years until our marriage broke up. In those four years we did have good times and seemed happy. We would work the yard together, we would go wood cutting together, we would take morning tea or sometimes have a BBQ. But we never went out together, there was no affection, no intimacy, he was the provider, but his life was with his mates, and I was the Mum at home, it became very lonely.

Charlie and the boys would play cricket in the backyard or over in the oval across the road. We would visit his mother each weekend. Christmas was good, the boys started high school during this time. Jayne was in late primary school. It is where I started my nursing career.

However, it was during this time that we started to drift apart and the problems crept in. This led to the break-up of our marriage, the boys were in their teens, had left school and were working and Jayne was in primary school.

When Charlie and I separated, because we were buying the house it had to go through the legal system. I explained to the kids what was happening and that I was leaving and that they could come with me or stay with their father. The boys, because of work, stayed with their Dad, and Jayne wanted to come with me.

Then things went terribly wrong. Charlie came home drunk one night and we argued. I ended up battered and bruised. So, both separation and assault charges went through the court at the same time. I left Orange three weeks later when and went to Sydney for three weeks with my tail between my legs and feeling ashamed and broken.

I made contact with the boys three weeks later. I eventually rang my sister and asked if I could come up there. No one was happy with me, and I get that now but at the time I was pretty messed up. I then moved to Newcastle.

Looking back, life when the kids were young was tough and I had little support from Charlie. There were a lot of good points in our marriage, great points.

We loved each other dearly, we were two broken people thrown into a situation that neither of us was ready for. Charlie wanted a mother, not a wife and I wanted a husband to love me. He simply didn't know how to show or give affection and in some things neither did I, our marriage was empty of that. We became two different people on different paths. We were both too young when we married, immature in our responsibilities as husband and wife and as parents.

It was years later I was told by Brett that when I left his whole world fell apart, he told me that if I'd stayed in Orange he would have been okay. Little did I know that this would be the start of his horrid journey with his mental health. It was a horrible time for all of us. Words we speak, actions we take destroy lives and I wounded these three precious lives that would take them years to heal.

Working Life and my Nursing Career

My first job was at Myers in the fruit and veggie department when I was 15 in 1969.

I then got a job at Coles Deli in 1972. I had a great boss and it was a fun time. Jeff was a baby. Mum and Maddy babysat. I didn't stay in that job long because I missed my Jeff too much. I just wanted to be his Mumma.

Following that, I had a job at Compak Welders in 1974. They made air compressors, battery chargers etc for businesses. I worked down the back with the men on the huge lathe. I learnt how to put the threads on either end of the long steel rods. They had to be perfect, and you needed a sharp eye to get that thread the exact length, they would then go through the bender to make handles for the battery chargers. I loved it, it was really good. Julia worked there too; up the top bolting the handles onto the battery chargers. Maddy ended up in the same section as Julia. I was the only female who worked with the men on the lathes. Maddy babysat my boys for me while I worked. She wanted a job, so I got her to apply for work here and I resigned to stay at home and be a mother to my two boys. Maddy got a job working with Julia. In 1985, at 32, I became an aged care nurse, attending lectures at Calare Nursing Home. My certificate says, 'Has proved proficient in all aspects of Nursing Care and Fire Procedures.'

My Nursing Career Achievements

1985: In-Service Training Certificate. Conform Management Consultants. LTD.

1991: Certificate in Palliative Care. Toronto Private Hospital Staff Development Program.

1992,1993: Certificate in Back Pain and Injury Prevention. Hunter Retirement Living.

1992: Certificate of Merit. Assistant in Nursing. Hunter Retirement Living.

1992: Certificate in Mental Health Skills in Caring for the Aged. Hunter Institute of Mental Health.

1993: Certificate in OH&S Workplace Committees. NSCA (National Safety Council of Australia).

1993: Certificate of Completion. Activity Education Programme. Hunter Volunteer Centre.

1994: Certificate of Completion. Advanced Activity Officer Education Programme. Hunter Volunteer Centre.

1994,1995: Games Workshop. Activity Officers Programme. Hunter Volunteer Centre.

1994: Certificate of Merit. Meeting Maslow's Higher Order of Needs - Activity Officers Course. Hunter Retirement Living.

1994: Certificate of Cultural Awareness and Workshop with Non-English-Speaking People. Migrant Resource Centre.

1996: Certificate in OH&S Accredited Course. Work Cover NSW.

1996: Retail Pre-Vocational Program. Orange SkillShare, OCTEC Inc.

2001: Certificate of Attendance. The TECH approach to Dementia Care. CCA (Catholic Care for the Aged) Staff Development Unit, Sandgate.

2003: Certificate III Community Services (Aged Care Work)

— Assistant in Nursing. Catholic Care of the Aged. July 3.

2003: Certificate III Community Services (Aged Care) Nursing Assistant Oct. 20. CCA.

2003: Certificate of Proficiency in Aged Care. Traineeship completed October 30.

2004: Certificate in Palliative Care Volunteer Training. Respite Volunteers for Palliative Care in Maitland Inc.

2005: Certificate of Appreciation in Well Ways: A traveller's guide to well-being for families of people with mental illness. Mental Illness Fellowship Victoria.

2006: Certificate in Senior First Aid. St Johns.

2007: Certificate of Appreciation from Dial-an-Angel. In recognition of her enthusiasm, loyalty, and diligence. This conscientious attitude earns our appreciation.

2008: Certificate Award. Angel of the Month, in appreciation of loyalty, dedication and the pursuit of excellence in your endeavours. Dial-an-Angel.

2008: Certificate of Appreciation. Angel of the Year. Loyal and diligence. Dial-an-Angel.

2008: Certificate in Teacher's Aide. Two-year correspondence course. CENGAGE Education.

2010: Certificate in OHS Consultation. Four-day course. Work Cover NSW.

2010: Certificate of Achievement. Low-Risk Theory and Practical Driving Course. WHEELS-SKILLS Pty Ltd. Skills needed to drive the bus in the Group Homes.

I was a stay-at-home Mum at that time and when Jayne started primary school, the boys were in high school. I made it a family discussion at the table that 'this is what I've decided to do, and I want your approval.'

I had no nursing background, I just walked into Clare Nursing Home and asked to see the DON (Director of Nursing) or deputy DON. I said I wanted to be a nurse and that I had no training.

I was interviewed and they said they would give me a three-month trial. I was called back to the office in three months for an appraisal. Both the DON and the deputy DON said, 'Well Lyn, what can we say?' I'm thinking 'oh dear'. They said 'You walked into Clare Nursing Home off the street wanting to nurse with no experience and you'd swear you'd been nursing for years. You ooze with confidence.' I thought 'Wow, I did not know that.' Amazing!

I was also lucky enough to train as an assistant to the physiotherapist. Pat Ringland was one of the best physios in Orange at the time. It was a privilege to be trained by her and work alongside her for three years. I worked three days as a physio assistant and nursed on weekends. I struggled at first to get my head around the order of things as the other girls were so fast and quick at their work. Finally, I got it together by watching and learning how the other girls worked, became efficient in my work ethic and remained that way for my working career and beyond.

I was also praised for my ability to change hats with no problem from physio assistant to nurse on weekends. And there my nursing career started!

After three years I left due to my marriage breakup. It was such a bonus to have that physio training. I was able to use that over the years in other nursing homes.

Leaving Orange

Jayne and I lived at Cams Wharf with my sister Julia and her family for a bit, then moved into a flat in Nords Wharf for six months before moving to Cooranbong. Jayne attended Avondale High School and we lived in Cooranbong for two years. My sister Julia got a job at the Big Prawn truck stop on the Pacific Hwy not far from Nords Wharf. I managed to get work there also even though I had to travel from Cooranbong.

There was a restaurant where the truckies stopped for meals. There was also a shop where you could buy your fresh fish and prawns. They also supplied bulk chips and chat potatoes for restaurants.

I worked in the shop, serving at the counter and selling fresh fish and prawns and did all the sorting of the potatoes cutting them into chips putting them in big plastic tubs and putting the chat potatoes in another. I then had to fill the tubs up with water and throw in a couple of big scoops of acid to keep the potatoes white. I wouldn't touch chips from a shop for a long time after knowing they were kept white using acid. This was the preparation for getting them ready to be transported to the restaurants without having them go brown. I loved this job!

One day the boss decided I would do better in the restaurant serving the truckies.

I guess wearing halter-neck tops showing bare arms and

having big boobs didn't help. It was money for him. He said, 'I want you in the restaurant.'

I said, 'I'm not going to the restaurant, I don't want to work there. I love it here in the shop.'

He said, 'give it a go.' So, I relented even though it went against the grain.

I was only there for a brief time because of the sleaziness of the men in that place ... and I just said 'Nope, not gonna happen' I had a fight with the boss and told him what he could do with his truck stop and walked out.

In 1991 while still at Cooranbong I decided to go back into nursing. I got a job at Carey Bay Nursing Home as the physio assistant.

I was under the supervision of a physiotherapist who came out to the home once a week and checked on the work she had me attend to. It was a good job and I liked it. I did a lot of foot and hand care, and range of movement with the residents' limbs, walked them using their frames, and got along with and worked well with all the staff. Occasionally I would fill in and do a nursing shift.

I became good friends with one lady in particular, Maree, she was wonderful. I was there for a year when the deputy DON applied for the DON position at Garden Suburb Nursing Home, Myall Rd. She got the position as DON and took me with her to train as an activities officer.

Working in Nursing Homes

In 1993 I did the Activity Officer course and in 1994 I completed the advanced Activity Officer course. In the activity role, I did physio. One of the kitchen staff who later became my colleague was a lovely lady named Marlene. She was a good swimmer and had swum many races in Lake Macquarie which became an asset later on when we ran a hydrotherapy program. We hit it off and made a great team.

The Nursing Home had an onsite bus. The DON approached me and asked if we could start a hydrotherapy program for some of the residents. We were able to take six of our residents to Valentine hydrotherapy pool for therapy sessions.

Marlene was keen on helping me. She had the strength to help load and unload the bus and help me with the hydraulic lift to lower the residents into and out of the pool. We had two residents who were great swimmers, one female being a gold medallist from Germany in her younger days, and the other a male a very good swimmer (who was a below-knee amputee). After our therapy time in the pool, it was time for games and a bit of fun before going back to the Nursing Home.

One year in the mid-90s the Olympic Games were on so us three activity officers decided we would create our own. We had swimmers (naturally, as we had these two, one being a gold medallist in her day!)

I modified a game of carpet bowls for residents in wheelchairs. We had swimming and cooking events. The other two AOs did the cooking and made cakes they entered, plus other activities. We had certificates made with gold, silver and bronze medals which Marlene was able to find. Marlene coordinated the swimming and I did the carpet bowls. One of the other activity officers made the certificates. Marlene had the medals on ribbons. There was a lot of excitement and buzzing in the lead-up to the games.

After the day of the games, we were able to get an ex-Australian gold medallist who came out to the nursing home and did the medal presentations, gold, silver and bronze. The lady who was the champion (from Germany) got the gold medal. The male amputee swimmer got the silver. The third swimmer received his/her bronze medal. We wheeled the three champions out the front in their wheelchairs. The Australian Olympic Games champion put the medals over their heads and gave an amazing speech, there were tears of joy, you could have sliced the air with a knife.

All the other residents got a certificate for participation and were pleased with their achievement. The emotions in the room that day were running high for residents and staff alike and many tears! The resident who got the gold medal for swimming had a heart attack a few days later and died. 'Well done' I say, the fact that she participated in the Nursing Home Olympic Games in her 90s was enough and then to go out with a gold medal was a blast!

Another time a Resident's Ball had been organised for various nursing homes, so preparation was on its way, and we needed to practise our wheelchair dancing. I had never done this before, so it was a lot of fun learning to wheelchair dance with the residents to old-time waltz music.

I did many other activities, I was the resident game board as I made many of my own games and modified others. I had them painting and pasting. I would sit for hours on my living room floor cutting, pasting, and sewing, to make floor games. All just to put a smile on their faces, this was the joy of working as an AO. We went all out for the Melbourne Cup, Easter, Christmas, and everything else in between. I had some great times and some interesting times working at Garden Suburb. While working there I found a house at Boolaroo to be closer to work and so it was a big move from Cooranbong to Boolaroo. My sister Julia and her husband Steve helped me move. I was at Boolaroo for three years. I didn't see Jeff then but Brett did come to stay for a bit. He made the move to Darwin while staying there with me.

In 1995, a full-time job as an activity officer at Cessnock House Nursing Home came up so I left Garden Suburb. There were 30 residents in the home and I used to care for three groups of residents. The first group sat up at the front of the house in the little sitting area. In the middle of the building, you had another little sitting area and a second group of residents. And you'd have the dementias down the bottom lounge room where I would do massages, foot, and hand care with them, as well as music therapy. In the front and middle areas, the residents liked to play games.

The first thing they loved to do was read the obituaries. That's what they all liked, in all the nursing homes I worked in. 'I've got the newspaper today, what do you wanna hear?'

'The obituaries! Just want to make sure our names are not there.' We did a lot of other activities as well. I discovered that one lovely lady was deaf and mute. One day I asked her if she would teach me sign language. She agreed. She used to teach in Newcastle in the School for the Deaf and Blind back in the day. And so my training began.

We would go down to the bottom lounge where it was quiet and she taught me. It was wonderful to communicate with her in a way I never knew how to before.

One day she became ill and the doctor was called. He couldn't understand her, so I was called in to liaise between her and the doctor. How cool was that! What a pleasure it was to have a resident teach me! And then use that skill to help her in time of need. I had some wonderful times at Cessnock House. Then things changed.

I'd only been there six months. One morning I walked into work and was fronted by the RN (Registered Nurse). I was verbally attacked with all the foul language she could lay her tongue to in front of the residents, at the top of her voice. She accused me of being lazy and said I did nothing with the residents. One AO with 30 residents was really hard, as I was used to sharing the load with other AOs. I was like a stunned mullet, my whole body just went limp.

When she walked away, one of the ladies said to me, 'Oh Lyn, I'm so sorry that that happened to you, she should never have spoken to you like that.'

I walked down to the other sitting area … no residents. I thought 'Why aren't they here?' I went out to the activity room where my office was, and there they all were. The little dementias, crying, and making a lot of noise. I walked in to hear 'Oh Lyn, you're here,' cried the residents. 'Take us out! We don't know why we're here.'

The staff had to put all the residents in this large room. This was ordered by the RN who abused me. All that did was confuse and upset them. They had their special place and just wanted to go back to where they were happy. And I lost it. When I looked at the residents I thought, 'Who are these people, I don't know them.' My brain fried!

The payroll officer heard what was going on and organized me to get a doctor's certificate the next day and bring in my resignation the following Monday which I did. He was very good and kind to me. And so, l left. I had only been there six months.

My doctor 'suggested going on antidepressants.' I didn't want drugs but knew I was not good. So, she gave me a sample, and it came with a cassette tape, and she said, 'I want you to listen to the tape'.

That was at Blackalls Park. I had moved from Boolaroo and now lived at Kurri Kurri about a forty minutes' drive away. It took me about 30 minutes to get to Freemans Waterhole.

The tape was counselling sessions on this particular medication. It was conversations between patients, psychiatrists and psychologists.

By the time I got to Freemans Waterhole, I knew what I needed to do and took the medication. I said to myself, 'Girl, you're sick and you need this medication' so I took it.

I knew that they were a bandaid effect and that I needed counselling to get me through, and that's what I did. I was nearly a year on sick leave before I could return to work. The storms in life are tough sometimes but you have to get up and soldier on.

Although I didn't think I would get up this time.

I swore I'd never be an activities officer again. I lost all motivation to do a lot of things. That was the end of 1995. I did eventually move forward and chose community nursing after that and loved it. But never activities!

Tough Times for our Family

While living in Cooranbong and working as a physio assistant at Carey Bay Nursing Home, Jayne and I were not getting along. I didn't know how to deal with the situation. I became frustrated and she was hurting. So, I thought it best that she went home to her father, however, things didn't work out with her father's new wife, Jayne's step-mother.

Jayne's life changed dramatically. She became a street kid and got into drugs. She became a lost soul. My heart aches, my guilt rises, and I pray to God for forgiveness for wounding the lives of my three children.

My boys came up to visit me when I lived at Cooranbong, but they didn't stay. They ended up in a caravan park for a while then moved on. Tough times were all around us, dark clouds lurking.

Brett came to me two years after the marriage breakup, he was 18 and he said, 'Mum I understand why you left, Dad and I hold no grudge.'

There was little contact with Jeff. He was hurting and kept it deep inside. We all struggled at that time. I think he built up a wall of resentment toward me. And I get that too. It was in 2020, Brett said again, 'I didn't have a problem with you going Mum, I understood that, but had you stayed in Orange, I would've been okay.' Then both boys would have had a home to come to, somewhere to sleep and eat.

I felt the guilt of my own parenting again. It was a time in my life that I was selfish and self-centred. And if I had to be honest, I felt I was the only one that was hurting. There were five people in this family and all five got stung by the pain of separation. I walked a lonely road to healing. Today I praise God for His faithfulness to forgive and take that guilt away and wash me clean. And take care of my children, God saw the pain in each one of us.

When I look back now, I think that it may have been the start of Brett's mental health issues. While still married and living as a family, I had stability and structure in an ordered household with mealtimes, bath times, bedtimes and every other time. I was very OCD! Everything had to be in order, that's how I had to live.

When I left, their father kicked the boys out and Brett's world fell apart. Brett was probably bipolar then, but no one knew it. Brett mentioned a man who he said took him in and said, 'if it wasn't for him, I would've been dead.' He said the family took him in and gave him guidance. To me, that was a real blessing. God continued to be over the lives of my children in their dark valley.

I struggled as a parent trying to love my three children. They were all different and needed to be treated differently and desperately needed to be loved, just as I did. I weep as I write this. I managed the house and took care of the physical needs, but the emotional needs were hard. My mother was the same, she could take care of the house and the physical, but not the emotional. At the end of the day, we both gave all we had, we did the best with what we had.

At Boolaroo, two years after Jayne had been in Orange, she rang me a couple of times to ask if she could come home.

I told Jayne that her behaviour would not be tolerated, she would get angry and hang up.

She was 16. It was coming up to Christmas and I had arranged to go to Coffs Harbour to spend Christmas and New Year with my sister Jazz and her husband. Jayne rang again and said, 'Mum I need to come home.' I could hear she was distraught. I told her about my trip and to ring me back in half an hour. I rang my sister Jazz and told her the situation and she said, 'so what's the problem? Bring her with you.' When Jayne rang back, I said, 'pack your bags you're coming home'. I could hear the weight of her stress fall off her shoulders. We had a lovely Christmas that year.

Jazz made her a lovely outfit for Christmas, I bought her some nice jewellery. That year,1993 was my 40th birthday. We had a great time in Coffs Harbour. Jazz had organised a party on New Year's Eve with Neil in charge of the big barbecue. There were lots of people with families arriving from the Orange and Cessnock areas. It was a great night! Well, some dilemmas, but it was great nonetheless.

Having Jayne at home had its challenges but mostly it was a delight to have her with me. I had learnt from my nursing days and professional help that you 'go where they're at, don't retaliate.'

We would sit on the floor and chat. I would ask her about her life on the streets and how she lived where she slept. She would open up and tell me about her life as a street kid. When I left Boolaroo to go to Kurri for work, she went to live with her boyfriend David whom she ended up marrying years later, they always stayed together. I'm so proud of her for that. It was something her mother couldn't do.

So, I packed up once again and moved to Kurri to be closer to my job in Cessnock, that was 1995. I got a private rental from a lovely lady. A lovely two-bedroom unit. I had a lovely pot garden on my veranda and thought 'this is it!' I was prepared to stay for quite some time. As it turned out that wasn't to happen. There was another move ahead.

In March 1996 I was contacted by my sister Maddy with the news of Mum not being good and that Julia and I needed to get to Orange asap. Julia picked me up and we travelled to Orange on Thursday arriving at 5:30pm. When we got to the nursing home, Jack and Maddy were by Mum's bedside. This was the same nursing home where I did my training to become a nurse.

Our mother was taken from her single room and placed in the dining room which was also used as a chapel. I was upset by that until Maddy told me the reason was that her room wasn't big enough to have any more than two chairs. I guess I should be grateful that we did have comfy chairs to sit on. I still was not happy that it was the dining room.

We sat around Mum holding her hand and talking to her and chatting to each other. Mum was struggling with her breathing, she seemed stressed, we were stressed. At 4am Friday morning 15 March 1996 our mother took her final breath. We left the home and went back to Maddy's house which was out of town, Jack went back to his home in Milthorpe not too far from Maddy. We spent our time together grieving Mum and going through her photo albums. Late Saturday evening we got another blow that our brother's son had taken his own life.

A month before mum's death I decided to ring Maddy and asked, 'have you organised Mum's affairs?'

She said, 'no I haven't'. Maddy was pretty stressed, she had full care of Mum's personal things, and her finances as well as her three boys to look after. I decided to help her. I drove down to Orange for a few days.

Mum wanted to be cremated like her mother, so we went to the cemetery and found where Grandma was placed in the wall. Next to Grandma's plaque was another lady and next to that was an empty spot. Twenty years after Grandma died there was still an empty plot, one space away from her! I said to Maddy, 'let's go and buy it, that belongs to Mum, it's got her name on it.' So, we went in and organised the plot and for two plaques.

Mum had left enough money to redo her mother's plaque as well, so we did that too. We chose the ones with little vases in them so you can put flowers in. It was like a heavy weight was lifted off Maddy's shoulders and mine. She was just so relieved to have it all organised.

The Sunday after our loss we rang the pastor of the SDA church in Orange to make the funeral arrangements. It was a very sad time for each of us. We spent Sunday with Jack comforting one another. We had to put Mum on the back burner to be with Jack and to try and make sense of this second tragedy.

We believe that it was Mum's death that took its toll on Jack's son. He loved her dearly. We all went into shock! Jack was a mess.

When the pastor arrived to make the arrangements, he was shocked to be told that we had another death in the family over the weekend. The church did not hesitate to take care of Jack's son as well. So, we buried Mum on Monday, 18th and our nephew on Thursday, 21st of March 1996. This was one horrific week, to say the least!

After a couple of weeks, I went back to Kurri. Jack wasn't doing well, and neither was I. I was still struggling with depression.

My sister Jazz rang me and suggested I move back to Orange and be a comfort to Jack (I don't think I was much help). And my next move began.

I packed up at Kurri, gave my furniture to Jayne and only had enough things to pack into Jack's ute and head back to Orange. I moved in with Jack at Milthorpe (June 1996). My depression became worse and I had become suicidal. This is when my counselling begun. It was here that Brett had his first breakdown in 1997 and came to live with Jack and me. Both '96 and '97 were difficult years.

In 1998 Brett and I were still living in Milthorpe with Jack. It was a challenging time as Jack was still dealing with the loss of his son and the whole situation was stressing him out. We were three cracked people in one house. I was still struggling from depression and Brett was recovering from his first breakdown. It was crazy.

I had started intense counselling and had three different counsellors altogether. They were brilliant. They all had their own technique and walked me through three different stages. Their counselling was a significant help to me. After that came to an end I decided to do something I had never done before, get my certificate in retail. I got some practical experience in a chemist shop, but it didn't progress further, I think because there were still a lot of stresses going on around me. It was a wonderful experience and good to do something different. I eventually went back to nursing.

I started community nursing in Orange with Wontama Nursing Care. I was working in Orange and travelling back and forth from Millthorpe 26km each way while trying to care for Brett as well as working split shifts attending to clients. I'd go in to do my morning shift then drive back to Millthorpe to attend to Brett, then back to town to do the afternoon shift. It was a struggle at times. Every day Brett felt that I was leaving him each time I'd go off to work and each time I explained to him that wasn't the case.

After a fall out with Jack, Brett and I moved into a two-bedroom unit in Orange. I was happy in Orange and in this unit. I had a great job and the unit looked lovely. I had lovely art deco furniture that I'd bought from an op shop.

Brett had more freedom in town and more people to hang around with. I encouraged him to help with meal preparation as otherwise he would sit in the lounge all day. He was skipping medication and tensions began developing in our relationship. I had been back and forth to the hospital with him and the mental health team were involved. He was challenging to say the least. I thank God for His guidance and strength and patience needed to handle many of his situations.

Brett had started to become abusive and one day he

threatened me. He told me I needed a good hiding and I just looked at him and said, 'Go ahead and make my day, but make it quick.'

With tears in his eyes he said, 'I can't, you're my mother and I love you but I'll pay someone $100 to hurt you.' I wasn't scared of him but had to keep in mind the words he was using seriously. I was in contact with the mental health team about Brett and his threats. I couldn't make him leave, the mental health team felt I was unsafe at home with him and recommended that I move interstate. To leave meant I had to break my lease, leave a fantastic job I loved, and give up my unit and all that I bought from the op shop, it was very upsetting. My doctor, who was a mental health doctor, felt the same way, and said to me, 'Lyn, you need to go interstate.' And that's how I ended up in Queensland.

My brother Tom came and helped me move my things into storage. I just kept the essentials, my white goods and all other personal stuff and gave the furniture and most of the small stuff away with two big bags of clothes. I put the word out to friends and they came around to take what they wanted. I remember while I was packing up sitting on the floor in my bedroom I was crying, and I looked up and said, 'God why do you hate me so much?' I sobbed and sobbed.

I packed my car, gave the keys to the storage shed to my younger sister, and drove away.

Moving to Queensland 1998

Sunshine Coast

I made the move to Queensland. I had previously lined up a place to stay in Buderim with friends there. I enrolled at Caloundra TAFE to start a Cert III in Aged Care. I got two assignments done while living with my friends. I was told a few weeks later that I needed to leave as the friends wanted their spare room for visitors. I packed my car and left with nowhere to go.

On my way into Caloundra, I noticed a Seventh Day Adventist Aged Care Retirement Village and decided I would apply for a job. Being an AIN, I didn't think I would have a problem getting a job there. So, I went in, and spoke to the receptionist and she said, 'there's nothing going at the moment', so I told her my story, and how I was now homeless. She said she was renting one of the cottages, and that it could be sold over her head overnight. However, she said 'I've got a camp cot and you're welcome to come and stay with me.' So that was my bed every night for three weeks, I lived out of my car throughout the day and went to TAFE and met the tutor in the park to get my assignments done. I was grateful to God for taking care of my needs.

I signed up at a nursing agency group in Maroochydore and managed to get enough work to keep me going, I was also on the dole. When I got tired, I would go and park my car somewhere and nap. Every day was a worry not knowing what each day would bring, but I had a bed at night and that made things easier.

Three weeks had gone by and still I had nowhere to live or a more permanent job. One evening as I sat in my car near the beach the sun was going down, people were scurrying to get home; I realised for the first time in my life I was homeless. I thought of my kids and remembered the times they had faced homelessness and uncertainty, and I understood then what they must have gone through, and my heart ached for them. As I turned to look down to the water God showed me the *Footprints in the Sand*, I remembered this poem from a child. That when there are two sets of footprints, He was walking beside you, and when you only saw one set, He was carrying you. God then took me back to my childhood and showed me how He carried me and loved me all through my life, the dark valleys, and the storms.

All I could say was 'You carried me and You never let me go' I just sobbed. I knew that my faith had been restored. I prayed for a miracle, a job, and a home to live in.

I knew I couldn't stay at the Village indefinitely and needed to find a more permanent place to stay. Some friends of mine in Brisbane had let me know about a flat to rent. I was still studying, and nursing part time for the agency at Maroochydore. I drove down to Brisbane and my boss rang me on the way. She asked me to come in and see her when I returned from my rental search as she had a job that she thought I'd be interested in. I got to the flat as suggested, I had a look through. It was dark and dingy, and I knew I couldn't live there. I went back to my car and reversed into a tree. The bumper bar was hanging off, so I pulled over at a servo on my way back to see if they could secure it enough away from the wheel so I could still drive.

I drove back to Maroochydore to see my boss. She told me about a family out at Blackall, western Queensland which was a 12 hour drive from Brisbane.

I was given the description of the job. A family living in Blackall were looking for a live-in carer/companion for their elderly mother who refused to go into a nursing home and didn't want to die in a hospital. My boss thought I was well suited for this job. She told me the job would involve caring for the lady who was on oxygen and wearing a nasal cannula 24/7 with a lot of medications. I would get a full wage; my own quarters separate from the house off the back where the two verandas joined by a small bridge. I would pay no rent, and my meals were provided for. I would eat with Mrs Walker and all food expenses were paid. I only needed to buy my own personal items. Wow! What an answer to prayer! God is good.

I had my interview in Brisbane with Mrs Walker's daughter Jennifer and got the job. I arranged the three quotes for my car and the repairperson. Left my car with the lady that kindly gave me a bed to sleep in and packed my bags ready for my new adventure.

Blackall Western Queensland

It was October 1998 when I boarded the bus and headed for Blackall. I was totally exhausted when I got on the bus and just sat back and said 'God, I have no idea where I am going or what I am doing, but You know, and faith is all I have to hang on to.' I collapsed in my seat and just enjoyed the trip. We stopped along the way or drove through Dalby, Miles, Roma, Mitchell, Morven, Augathella then Blackall. What a great trip!

When I got off the bus in Blackall the daughter Cheri, was waiting for me. I remember her saying to me, 'You must be Lyn.' I smiled and said, 'how can you tell?' she smiled back and said, 'I can just tell, you look exhausted.' She took me to the home I would be staying in for the next eight months. I met Mrs Walker, and then settled. It was a pleasant meeting. I was able to rest up for the rest of the day and start my new job the next morning.

A system was set up for Mrs Walker to use when she needed assistance. It was a battery-powered doorbell with two parts. I had the bell part which I could carry around in my pocket and if Mrs Walker needed me, she would just press the button and I would be there to attend as needed. It was a good system and worked well.

Mrs Walker had five adult children. Walker was my maiden name, and my Mum had six adult children, so I thought that was interesting. What are the odds! The house was a beautiful old Queenslander on a big double block with huge verandas, lots of palms and ferns in pots on tall stands on the verandas. The floorboards were all polished. They had renovated the flat before I arrived, polished the boards, put air con in. Lovely old furniture and linen sent out from Brisbane for my bed. It was just lovely!

The job could be challenging at times. Mrs Walker and I had an argument one night over something silly. Once we got through that barrier of who we were, two stubborn and independent women we became friends despite our differences and worked well together.

Just before Christmas I got a call from Jazz, my sister, to tell me her husband Neil had been diagnosed with terminal cancer and didn't have long to live. I was devastated. I told her to keep me updated.

In the meantime, my hosts made Christmas special for me because I was so far from home and because of the bad news I had received from my sister. They put on a wonderful big spread for Christmas, an abundance of food and bought me beautiful gifts. It was just lovely and very thoughtful. I felt blessed.

It was January 1999 when I had a call from the mechanic to say my car was ready to pick up. So, it was back to the Sunshine Coast. I took the bus back, another long trip again. After I picked up my car, I packed it with a few things I'd left behind. I took off the next day, drove back to Blackall, and it was the best 12 hour drive I've ever had. I loved it, the open road, all by myself. Simply the best!

When I got back I realised my old car would not get me back to NSW when the job finished. I had to think about my next move and that was to get another car.

The family in Blackall gave me a week off to go to Coffs and spend time with my sister Jazz and her husband Neil. I went by bus to Brisbane and then flew to Coffs Harbour. My sister picked me up from the airport.

Neil stayed at home the whole time under the supervision of the palliative care team. Jazz had a lot of experience with nursing care and did pretty much what she wanted and needed to do for her husband, with the palliative care team by her side. When I arrived, I said to Neil with a grin on my face 'I'm just letting you know I'm not coming to your funeral when you're dead so I'm here for a week to spend quality time with you'.

'Good on you girl,' he said, 'I'd rather that than having you come when I'm not going to see you.' I had a wonderful week with him and my sister then it was back to Blackall. Four months later I got a phone call from my sister Jazz to say Neil had passed away that Friday night. I sobbed.

During my time there, I got to know Blackall and made new friends with Rod, the local paramedic and his wife. On my days off I explored the local area. I got to know a few people. I drove down to Tambo and bought a collectible Tambo Teddy. Rod, the paramedic who was in charge at the Ambulance Station, allowed me to tag along with him as a volunteer on my days off.

Mrs Walker wasn't too happy about that, she thought I should be spending 24/7 with her. I reminded her that I wasn't there to work seven days a week, that I needed two days off to have a break and do my own stuff.

I started my lessons in driving an ambulance. I'd already

had some practice reversing into narrow spaces using the mirrors and I really took to driving this big vehicle. So I passed the driving tests. Another test I had to do was CPR on a mannequin without missing a beat while the ambulance was swerving in and out of the trees on the side of the road. I passed even though it was hard. Trying to stay focused was hard when I kept losing balance.

One day Rod came and picked me up and said, 'I need you, there's an old gent who's passed out in the cemetery while visiting his wife's grave'. We got out there, got the old gent up off the ground and into the ambulance and Rod said, 'I've got to sit in the back with him, so you'll have to drive, we're going down to Tambo hospital.'

As I started up the ambulance, I didn't take into account the size and width of the vehicle and that you had to swing out to go around the corner. As I took off, I knocked down the headstone of some lady named Betty. Rod got out of the vehicle, scratching his head and said, 'well we can't do much about that at the moment so Betty will have to wait, and I'll fix her up when I get back'. I'm thinking 'oh dear, okay'. Anyway, we saw the funny side of it, had a chuckle and then got back in the vehicle and drove to Tambo.

The old gent was okay, he had just fainted from the heat and lack of water. He stayed at the hospital, and we headed back to Blackall. Rod did get back to fix the headstone I ran over, luckily it wasn't broken!

Mrs Walker played scrabble with her friends often, they would come around to the house once a week. One time one of the ladies couldn't make it so I was asked to sit in and play with them. Very enjoyable!

She loved her garden, she grew roses. We often went out in the yard so she could attend them. I would have to connect her cannula to the mobile oxy tank that was on wheels and off we'd go. Cheri would come in often to check on things and occasionally her son Butch would pay a visit.

Another time Mrs Walker wanted to change her will. The solicitor came out and he was going through the will with her. I had been outside to give them privacy. I walked in later and looked down, and here's the solicitor standing at the table discussing Mrs Walker's will while he's standing on the cannula hose. I looked up at him and said 'Well this is interesting, you're standing on the cannula. Not a good look while the will is being changed'. We all laughed.

Mrs Walker had begun showing signs of weakness, her cannula kept falling out and she seemed to be struggling to breathe. I rang the ambulance and they came and took us to Tambo hospital. She had a heart attack. The doctor told her she was dying and asked what treatment she wanted. She said she wanted no resuscitation and wanted to go home. Her daughter Jenny, in Brisbane, came out to stay with us. Jenny did the night shift and I did the daytime caring for her mother. So, she was put back in the ambulance and taken home where she was well cared for.

I had taken myself out to Longreach for the day, leaving Jenny with her mother and another carer who came to fill in for me sometimes. I had a great run looking at the old machinery on the side of the road. I went through the Stockman's Hall of Fame and had a good look around, I thoroughly enjoyed it. Very hot though, 45 degrees.

While having a great time, the time had finally come for me to look for another car. I went out to Longreach Wednesday and signed up for a brand new Daihatsu Terios and had to pick it up the following Tuesday. I'd been out at Blackall for about eight months at that stage. That Sunday morning after my trip to Longreach, I woke early that morning and suddenly realised there'd been no bell ringing from Mrs Walker.

As I walked into her bedroom, I could not see her at first, there was no hose running across the floor to the bathroom, so I knew she wasn't there. I stepped further into her room and looked toward her bed and there she was, her cannula had fallen out of her nose, she had gotten out of bed and knelt down to pick it up and didn't have the energy to put it back in her nose let alone get back up.

She was kneeling with her head resting between the bed and the bedside table. I went into the side closed-in veranda where her daughter was sleeping and woke her and told her she better come quickly and told her what had happened. I asked her what she wanted me to do, and she said call the ambulance and Rod came. The police also had to be called because she had died at home.

It was an incredibly sad time for the family. I gave Mrs Walker a wash and changed her into a lovely long nightie that she had chosen, combed her hair and put a small posy of her own roses on her bedside table. She was now ready for when the family arrived at the house. A memorial service was arranged for the following Thursday.

Off to Longreach on Tuesday I went to pick up my new car and drive back to Blackall. The house was very quiet and I began getting my stuff sorted.

The Walker family was wonderful and allowed me to stay for a week while I got myself sorted. The following Saturday morning Jazz rang me to let me know Neil had passed the night before. I said to her, 'let me know when and what time the funeral will be'. On the day of Neil's funeral at 1 pm, I went to the park which had a lovely pond of water with a bridge over it. I went and stood there in silence for 20 minutes in respect for the family in their time of sadness. So, in one week, Mrs Walker died, I lost my wages, and I lost my brother-in-law. I had a $20,000 debt and no job. I stayed a few days at the house and then went to stay with Rod and his wife.

What could I do but to move on? I packed my new car, said my goodbyes, and drove out of town. I thanked God for my car with aircon and said, 'Lord, take me home' and off I drove. I was grateful for the experience I had in Blackall. I went back to the Sunshine Coast, picked up the few things I left there and then drove to Coffs Harbour on 19 July 1999, Jazz's 50th birthday. The new car was lovely to drive. I stayed with Jazz for just a few days. I really struggled with Neil's death and drove back to Newcastle to look for somewhere else to live and another job. All up I was in Queensland for about ten months. And what a joy it was, I felt richly blessed.

Moving back to the Hunter Region

Leaving Coffs Harbour, I headed back to Newcastle and stayed with my sister Julia and her family. I soon moved out to Rutherford in September 1999. I got a job with Catholic Care first and did community nursing at Rutherford before I took a position at Lochinvar Nursing Home and stayed there for two years. While I was at Lochinvar my husband died in 2001. Sad time for the kids and myself.

It was here that I would be taken on another journey. It had been three years since my mother died and I had not shed one tear. I became very fond of one of the nuns at the nursing home, Sr Mary, she had become very ill and was dying. One morning I came in to start a morning shift, I started my appointed work. While making one of the beds Rose came to tell me that Sr Mary was slipping away, and it would be nice if I went to pay her one last visit. I could not bear it and said, 'no I don't want to see her.'

I was becoming very emotional over this sad event. Rose came back a short time later to tell me that Sr Mary had just passed. Finally, I decided to go and say my goodbyes. As I was walking down the corridor I was thinking of my Mum and the closer I got to the room the more upset I became. Sr Catherine was just coming out of the room, and I told her that I hadn't cried for my mother for three years since her passing. She said, 'Lyn, go in and sit with Sr Mary, you need to do this'. When my mother died she was very agitated, her eyes had been fixed open for several days and her mouth wouldn't close. She was frantic, like fear had taken hold of her, it was horrid and distressing for us to watch her like this. But her heart kept pumping.

As I walked into the room toward Sr Mary, I looked at her and she was so peaceful. I took her by the hand and I thought of Mum's favourite song, *Softly and Tenderly Jesus is Calling*. I realized that I had put my mother in the place of Sr Mary and I sobbed and sobbed for the first time in three years I cried for my mother. God gave me the peace of this nun to replace the horror of my mother's death. It was so amazing! Bless You God for Your tender mercies!

At Lochinvar when someone dies the residents aren't locked away from the pathway that the deceased person is taken out. They are all gathered at the back entry door singing and the nuns praying while we all wait for the bed to be wheeled down the corridor led by the undertaker and the DON walking at the back of the bed. I'd never seen anything like this, paying respect to the residents waiting to farewell the passing of a friend . It was amazing.

As soon as I saw the bed and Sr Mary uncovered from the chest up with her rosary beads draped around her hand, coming toward the back door I broke down and sobbed. What a beautiful way to send off a resident from a nursing home where all the other residents get the chance to say goodbye. The singing continued until the hearse had driven away. Just beautiful!

My journey of healing from the grief of my mother's death didn't end there. Sr Catherine came to me and suggested that I finish my journey by taking part in the service itself, so I took part in 'covering and uncovering the Pall.' Through this experience, I was able to cry and grieve in a healthy manner that gave me healing. Sr Catherine and Sr Loretta were godly nuns.

When Lochinvar closed its doors, I was transferred to St Joseph's Nursing Home at Sandgate, along with some of the other staff. While working at St Joseph's I shaved my head for Canteen Kid's Cancer, three months before Jayne's wedding. I had a number three shave. Being the mother of the bride, I thought best to have some hair. Some didn't think I would go through with it but, I came back to the ward with a number three shave, after all, it was for kids with cancer. I raised $819 on my own with help from my family.

I spent three years at St Joseph's Nursing Home. While there I completed my Cert III certificate in aged care. I worked in a ward where we had three wings, they were behavioural wards. A lot of hard work, some good times and some unpleasant times. Made good friends and cared for many beautiful residents.

Nursing care was starting to fall below the standard of care it once was. Due to false accusations, a young trainee was used by management to set me up, she had no idea what was happening, she was as green as grass. I was suspended after that incident for a week. When I came back, I was given the same girl to work with again. I pulled her aside after our morning change over, she said to me, 'I had no idea you would be suspended' and she apologised. I told her that she had been set up by management, then I said, 'let's put this behind us and start again.' I introduced myself to her and said, 'let's go and have a great day' and we did. I put a two-week notice in a week later and a new direction was to begin.

I then started Community Nursing with Dial-an-Angel where I had a variety of roles in the community such as palliative care, dementia care/aged care, and childcare with a variety of disabilities. I had one live-in role for two years with an elderly man, a wonderful job and rewarding. I worked with another lady, Helen, on this job, it was great. We both stayed with him until he passed.

I also did a two nights-a-week sleepover in Forster with an elderly lady named Betty, she was a treat to care for. The clients lived mostly around the Newcastle area. Some of the clients with dementia could be difficult as they often wandered off or walked out the door and you would have to walk with them, so they didn't harm themselves or get lost. It was a challenge sometimes. It was important how you approached and talked with them, to bring them back. It wasn't always easy; you just needed the right person at the right time.

Dial-an-Angel became the agency for supplying nursing staff to the group homes, so I began my last job working in the group homes before my retirement. After a period, I impressed the manager with my work ethic, and she asked me one day 'When are you going to come and work for me?' and I said, 'when you advertise'.

She said, 'Well, it will be up shortly. You just make sure you don't miss it; I want that application in.' A couple of days later she was back in the home and asked me if I had filled out that application, so I applied and I got the job.

I was with Dial-an-Angel for maybe three years and had a great time, I learnt new skills and was blessed with broad experience. I was Angel of the Month twice, Angel of the Year once and also received a certificate of appreciation! It was important to get one of those certificates, I did not think I would make it!

That is how I left community nursing and went into working with disability in the group homes. I started working at the Bolwarra group homes first. I also worked at the Thornton group homes, which had two homes located on the same block.

I worked in both of these houses during my time there, although I spent more time in the back house. The front house was called 'Pinewood' and the back house was called 'Greenwood'). Great times and great staff! It was here in 2010 where I had my bus accident, broke my wrist while in the shower at home and required surgery that led to my retirement and a disability pension.

The nursing staff in the homes were great. I learned how to drive the buses, how to load and unload the clients in wheelchairs on and off the buses, and how to secure their wheelchairs properly with the straps. They were hard to handle with my arthritic hands, but I managed somewhat.

I had many achievements in my nursing career, including how to interact with people through my aged care nursing, community experience, and working with young people and children with disabilities. Working with the kids in the community was tough at times.

There were a variety of disabilities in the homes: bipolar, schizophrenia, cerebral palsy, many of the kids had seizures. There were five residents in each house. Working in the homes brought me up to retirement in 2010.

Life in Cooranbong

I had a friend in Cooranbong that I grew up with in the church in Orange. I hung around with her and went back to church for a couple of years while there. I spent a lot of time at her place. She was a mental health nurse and had been since she left school. One night Helen rang me and said, 'what are you up to?'

I said, 'I'm in bed Helen, it's eleven o'clock'.

She said, 'well come out, I've got six clients out the back of the hospital near the water. They have their tents; we'll have our tent. Come out and stay with us, I'm just taking them for a camp out overnight.'

So, I got up and off I went. I got there only to find out they were the six worst patients in the hospital. She said, 'Not to worry, that they're well medicated, I've given them their drugs.' Anyway, a friend of hers turned up on a motorbike who wanted her to go for a ride. So, she jumped on this motorbike and took off. Leaving me standing there with a big campfire and these six mentally ill male residents which she had just finished telling me they were the worst of the patients in the hospital, seriously!

Anyway, I stayed calm and managed to handle the guys well. Helen was gone for half an hour, and it felt like forever. The men did behave well during that time. They stayed close to their tents. It was a good night, and we had fun. The men had two tents with three men in each.

Helen and I shared a tent. The next morning Helen organised the boys with breakfast and had them help with packing everything up to go back to the hospital. Saturday night out spontaneously! The only way to go. I got involved working with Helen when she was working with the Salvation Army drug and alcohol rehabilitation farm which was out at Morisset. We went on outings together. I used to go out to Morisset Hospital and help her out on craft days on my days off while I was still working at Carey Bay Nursing Home.

When Helen worked at the farm, she was able to get the bus, and she'd take the boys out and I'd sometimes go with them. There had to be a nurse in the back with the boys if she was driving. They were a bit raw around the gills with the language but were pretty good. We always had a good time. I enjoyed working with Helen. I learnt skills in mental health not knowing that I would need to use them later on down the track.

A gospel singer from America, Michael Harris, was booked to do a concert in Australia at the Seventh Day Adventist Memorial Church in Cooranbong. Helen arranged for 20 of the guys from the Drug and Alcohol Rehab Farm to attend this concert. I volunteered to help with transporting the boys on the bus to the concert.

Michael told his life story and his journey, the drugs and alcohol the 'hip-hop' band he and his brother founded. And how God had led him out of the life of addiction to become a preacher of the gospel. He talked to them as a friend, sang to them and showed them the tracks up his arms where he had been shooting up. The boys just loved him! They cheered, whistled, and had a fun time.

Then another time an evangelist named Leo came out from America and gave a lot of his time out at the farm telling his story to both girls and guys of his rebellion, and how God showed him a better way, then called him to be a preacher. I volunteered at this event also. Today, only one of the boys who attended both these concerts gave his life to Christ and was baptised. Enduring many trials over the years, John is still in the church and is still faithful to his God.

My friend Tina and I went to America in 2011 to celebrate Leo's 50th. He was the evangelist who came over to the Rehab Farm. Tina and I joined Leo at the last stretch of his Walk across America event and were thrilled to walk the last mile with him to the beach of Coronado near San Diego. It was a great celebration.

When Tina and I left San Diego, we drove to La Sierra University for a tour but found it closed so we headed to Loma Linda University where we had the best tour by one of the doctors, what a treat! We had an enjoyable time there. I drove from there back to LA Where we boarded our plane to fly home. Great trip!

After completing his Walk across America event, Leo and his team then thought, 'What can we do next?' so they came up with a 7-day Mexican Riviera Cruise.

Jayne and I went on that cruise in 2012 which was fabulous. She had never been to the States. We flew to LA and hired a car. Jayne drove, she'd never driven on the wrong side of the road before, she did very well! We met another couple from Brisbane in LA as well, they were booked into the same motel as us. So, we did the trip to San

Diego together. We had a great trip. We arrived in San Diego staying at the Adventist Paradise Valley Retirement Village. We boarded the ship *Holland America* the next morning.

We spent seven days on the sea, and we had three port stops: Cabo San Lucas, Puerto Vallarta, Mazatlan. Mazatlan was cancelled due to a 'Warlords dispute' where there was a lot of gunfire. We were able to spend extra time at Puerto Vallarta. The tours were great! We went on a catamaran, Jayne did some snorkelling, never snorkelled before and she loved it. I got seasick and had to rest.

We did some shows on the ship, Jayne bought some art. We had a great time together, it was really, really good. Wonderful time sightseeing and shopping, making new friends, lots of laughter and dining together.

We sailed back to San Diego and stayed overnight at the Adventist Paradise Valley Retirement Village. Massive and spectacular! We hired an MG sports car, travelled back to LA and boarded our plane home. Great trip!

A Journey I Never Thought I Would Have to Take

Brett's Story

Brett struggled greatly with his mental health. He was non-compliant with his medications which caused many manic episodes and several stints in and out of the mental health clinics. Brett lacked confidence in himself and felt insecure. He was extremely sensitive and often emotional. His father rejected him at a young age. Brett had a strong desire to achieve in life. He completed many courses over the years and tried to better himself. He loved being a security guard. His hobbies were woodwork, metal work and he loved music. He had a guitar and a bass guitar and taught himself how to play and write music. He volunteered at FoodCare in Orange where he had various roles. He enjoyed talking to people, he was very caring and compassionate. It was never too hard for him to help someone. Brett has never been married, nor does he have any children. He has never been in a relationship but did have female friends.

Brett's Achievements in Education

I have found many of Brett's certificates in his belongings; he amazes me! He was a person with excellent work ethics and skills, and he had a fervent desire to obtain permanent employment and did everything he could to succeed. Unfortunately, his mental health got in the way of many of these tasks.

Here is a list of his certificates showing just how strong his desire was to persevere.

***

1990-1992: Retail Assistant. Franklin Supermarket. Retail and Dispatch, cash handling, stock replenishment. Brett was in his teens; this was his first job.

1993: skilled Gap Production Worker. Central West Group Apprentices LTD. Brett successfully completed this five-week course. Basic welding, computer knowledge, landscaping, plant and tree propagation. This was four years before his first major breakdown. He had that drive to succeed back then.

1998: Carpentry Falsework & Formwork Skills. He had six subjects and passed. Hunter Institute of Technology.

2002: Certificate III in Security (Guarding) Safecity Training Academy.

2002: Certificate II, Hostec Hospitality Services. (Alcohol & Gaming).

2002: Certificate of Completion – Baton & Handcuffs. Hunter Firearms Academy.

2002: Certificate III in Investigative Services (Private Agency Practice).

He didn't do too well in this course, although he did get one pass and one distinction. He withdrew and didn't complete this course. No matter how hard the course this boy was determined! And continued through his struggles with mental health. Well done I say!

2003: Certificate III in Security (Guarding). Chubb.

2003: Foundation and Vocational Education.

He may have struggled with this one as he didn't complete this course. Hunter Institute.

2003: In recognition of 100% attendance at Looking After Your Mental Health for 8 Sessions from October 9 until December 4. Supported Recovery Hunter Valley.

2003: Certificate of Participation. For participating in the Horticulture Program at Kurri Kurri TAFE, Hunter Health.

2005: OHS General Induction for Construction Work in NSW,WORKCOVER.

2009: Certificate of Achievement; Rank achieved; 8th & 9th grade. SHI-GAN TAEKWON DO AUSTRALIA.

2012: Certificate II in Security Operations. National Operations Training & Development. Competent in all units. 26/10

2013: Apply first aid, perform CPR, Provide basic emergency life support. Red Cross College.

2013: Certificate II in Security Operations. National Operations Training & Development. Competent in all units. 20/8

2013: Certificate II in General Education for Adults. Western College the advantage.

Brett fulfilled all requirements.

2014: Certificate in Hospitality-service of alcohol. DMP Training. 23/8

2014: Certificate in Hospitality-gambling service. DMP Training. 24/8

2014: National WHS General Construction Induction Training. NSW Work Cover.

2014: Certificate II in Construction; work safety in the construction industry. OCTEC Training Services.

2015: Family & Community Services; Housing NSW. "Dear Mr Brett Constable, Housing NSW would like to present you with this Certificate to show our appreciation for your efforts in maintaining your property to a very high standard." I am impressed. He was keeping his home in better order back then.

2015: Provide cardiopulmonary resuscitation, provide first aid. Royal Life Saving.

2016: Certificate II in Engineering. 16 UNITS; Competent in 7 units and withdrew from the rest. Metal & Engineering Training Package, Western Institute, Orange.

2017-2020: Statement of Attendance. Brett Constable has held a volunteer role with FoodCare Orange from 2017-2020. At FoodCare Brett Constable was part of a team of volunteers that operated a supermarket style shop for low-income families and individuals.

2018: Certificate III in Community Services. Competent in all units! Western Institute, Orange.

Brett struggled greatly with his mental health and in the middle of all that he achieved so much. All the above just shows how determined he was to ride above his challenges. Unfortunately, his life didn't pan out the way he had expected, his mental health and drug addiction took its toll on him for the worse.

Brett's first major breakdown 1997

It was one year after Brett's cousin's death in 1996 who suffered from mental health also. I think that may have been the trigger for Brett's mental illness to finally show through properly. The first breakdown occurred inside a video shop, Brett was 24 yrs old. He had locked himself in a hotel room and later decided to go for a walk. He walked to the other end of the main street (Summer St). Brett had had a destructive fallout with his father just before this happened.

He sat in the gutter outside the Blockbusters video shop, he told me he had been crying. One of the girls in the video shop saw him and noticed a knife in his boot and she called the police. The police came and spoke to him. He couldn't understand why, after all, he wasn't doing anything wrong. He said to me, 'couldn't they see that I was crying, I wasn't causing any trouble'. He got up and went into the video shop and they followed him. He went down the back of the shop to get away from the police and they cornered him. He went crazy and broke the back door trying to get away.

When he realised he had a gun pointed at his head he knew things weren't good. He said to the police, 'I don't want any trouble,' and he put the knife on the table and his arms in the air. It took six cops to get him in the paddy wagon.

He was taken to the Orange police station where they locked him in a cell for the night. The next day they had him transported to Long Bay Psychiatric Hospital in Sydney where he was diagnosed with Bipolar Affective Disorder.

Jack and I managed to see Brett on our way home from

Newcastle. We made arrangements to see him in Long Bay. Not without a fight though. I was put through many channels of rejection to get in. As his Mumma, I stood my ground like a bull at a gate until they relented. I got to see my Brett; it was the hardest dark tunnel I've had to walk in. He gave me the biggest bear hug.

Three weeks later he was transferred back to Orange to attend a court hearing, the judge tried to pin him with a speed high, Brett shook his head and said no. I learnt later that a 'speed high' and a 'manic high' are terribly similar.

The judge then ruled that he spend a month in Bloomfield Mental Health Clinic to be assessed. He was placed in my care on release from the clinic and he lived with my brother Jack and I in Milthorpe for the next 12 months.

The psychiatrist in Sydney had told me that Brett's brain had been fried and that he was in a bad way. They said that he should have been taken to Sydney straight from the video shop, not locked in a cell overnight with no care. Brett told me the police in Orange had tormented him all night. Hard stuff to swallow. I saw the damage as I cared for him, he was like a small child who couldn't function in any cognitive skills.

Second major breakdown 2001

While living in Bathurst Brett was once again very unwell. I didn't see him through this breakdown as I wasn't notified of its happening. I do know that it happened just before his father's death on 30 June 2001.

It wasn't until after the event that my sister Maddy and I picked him up to take him to his father's funeral. He was a mess, I can't describe it.

My heart aches as I write this. He later told me that he attempted suicide but failed. He stood on a box with the rope around his neck, then he just looked up and said 'God, there's got to be something better than this,' and he took the rope from around his neck.

Brett came and stayed with me after that for a little bit. He didn't live around me at this time, and I didn't spend a lot of time with him then, so I don't know a lot about this breakdown. I do know that it was pretty bad.

Third major breakdown 2003

Brett was living with me out at Rutherford when he started to get abusive and I told him to leave. And of course, I worried about him not knowing where he was.

He then rang me a few days later to tell me that he was living in a boarding house in Waratah, Newcastle. I paid him some visits and noticed he wasn't the best mentally. He told me he went to the Wallsend SDA church, and they were having communion, so they invited him to join in, I thought that was lovely. He took part in the foot washing and the unleavened bread and grape juice. He loved it.

I was again notified that he had been picked up by police, riding a bike, unfortunately naked on the streets of Waratah and was transported to the Mental Health Clinic in Watt Street. He told me his story, he went out to see if his clothes were dry on the line and saw a bike leaning up against the wall so he thought if the bike proved worthy, he would buy one like it for his nephew Joel. In his mind, a test ride was a must. I said to him that was well and good, but the neighbours didn't think naked was appropriate at the time.

I thought at the time this was the worst breakdown he'd had. When I saw him in the clinic I noted how childlike in his mannerisms he was, I mentioned it to the RN and she agreed. I thought there was no way this boy could care for himself, so I picked him up two weeks later and brought him home and cared for him for the next six years. We had some really good times together even though they were tough at times. For him anyway.

I was doing community care work at that time, live-in caring for an elderly gent three days a week. Brett wouldn't go out, he just laid on the lounge most of the time for those six years. I had to basically push him out the door to come and help me with shopping and visiting his sister and the kids. We eventually started to take it in turns to pay for lunch out every week. We both enjoyed those times together. He kept a lot of his thoughts to himself. We went out on a couple of New Year's Eves to Newcastle foreshore, we got the train in from Maitland (I'd leave my car at the station). We enjoyed the fireworks and music, a bite to eat then got the train back to Maitland and then home. The second time we went to Stockton where a girlfriend was singing, it was my 50th I think. It was a good night, we both enjoyed it.

2009/10 - Brett then decided that it was time to move out as he felt he couldn't live with his mother for the rest of his life. He said, 'if I don't try I'll never know if I can make it on my own'. It took me by surprise and I was saddened to see him go, but understood. He wanted to go out to a property my sister had been living on near Narromine. I managed by chance to get him the cottage she and her husband had.

So, the move began. Living with me he saved quite a bit of money which helped him to get his white goods, a bed and a TV and whatever else he needed.

It was good for a while but then the struggles started to dip in and he became depressed which became stressful for both me and him. He got a dog while there which was great company for him, he named him Tucker. Living here was a hairy ride for him to say the least, from floods to mice plague and contending with his mental health. I travelled out there every two weeks, taking care of things the best I could. A lot of stress and worry. I always made sure he had plenty of food, containers to keep food stuff in, towels, sheets, treats, toilet paper etc.

2012 - Brett decided to apply for public housing which was going to be a five-year wait. Too long I thought! I said to him 'What man says and what God says are two different things, let's pray about it.' We did, and in three weeks he had a two-bedroom house in Narromine. Prayer works and God is faithful. So his next move began. I helped him again with this move, another big job but we both got it done.

Brett stayed in this house for two years and his depression dipped in again. While here he got another dog and called her Lucy.

2014 - it got to a point that he couldn't care for the dogs, he started to neglect them until one day they both got out and ran away. They made their way to a property and killed nine sheep. The property owner went after them with his gun. He shot Lucy while she was in the dam and Tucker took off back home. The police went to Brett's place and told him what had happened; he was told that he would have to hand Tucker over to be put down. Brett signed him over to the ranger and Tucker was gone. Brett was fined $1800 dollars for the damages the dogs had caused. That was a hard blow to Brett, he started to go into deep depression from the grief of the loss of his two dogs.

Brett felt alone in Narromine and decided it was time to move on, he thought that maybe going back to Orange where he grew up was the way to go. The waiting period for housing this time was 10 years, which stressed him. He said he couldn't stay that long and he would end up dying.

So again, I said to him, 'What man says and what God says are two different things.'

We prayed and God stepped in again. With discussions and letters to Housing, he had a two-storey townhouse in three months. He wasn't sure if this was the right move but as he said, 'this is where all my problems started.' He thought if he went back to face the music he would come good.

Little did any of us know, especially him, that this move would be his worst nightmare! It was in Orange 2015 that he pushed me out of his life, and I didn't know when I would see or hear from him again. I sent texts to him but never got a reply. Four years went by.

Fourth Major breakdown
4 December 2019 to 23 January 2020

Again, Brett was having more struggles with his mental health as well as drug addiction and he was in a bad way. He had gone to his brother's place to get help. Because Jeff hadn't spent a lot of time with Brett he didn't understand Brett's ways or help language.

Jeff rang me and said he was hanging around his place and Karen and the kids were frightened. Brett was in need of help, he was asking Jeff to take him out the road, Jeff didn't understand what he meant. He rang me and I told him Brett was asking him to take him out to the mental health clinic. When Brett didn't get the help he needed he obviously went back to his unit.

So, Jeff went over to Brett's unit and offered to take him out to Bloomfield (mental health clinic). Brett refused the help and Jeff left. Jeff ended up ringing the police and Brett was found in a paddock just out of town sitting in a horse trough having a bath, he told me later that he hadn't had a shower in a few days so when he saw the trough full of water he thought 'I'll have a bath' and so he did. Made sense to me. He was upset that the police wouldn't let him put his boots on, I said to him, 'did they let you put your clothes on?' 'Oh yeah, I had my clothes on,' I said 'praise God!' (he makes me chuckle sometimes).

He was then taken to and admitted into Bloomfield Mental Health Clinic in December 2019 and discharged in January 2020, about a four-week stay I believe. During

Brett's time in the clinic my brother Tom suddenly died. My brother's death had such a devastating impact on Brett, not to mention our family. I told Brett that I would be in Orange for Tom's funeral and would come and see him at the clinic. I went to see Brett as I told him I would.

Seeing Brett in the clinic was quite a shock. He was devastated over his uncle's death, he wanted to go to the funeral but was not allowed. It was by far the worst state I'd ever seen him in. He was so thin, so drawn and wrinkled in his face, at first glance I didn't recognise him. I knew it was drug-related, something heavier than the marijuana he was using. He'd been addicted to marijuana for many years but this time he was different. It is hard to describe what he was like in writing. Words cannot convey how I felt and what he must have been going through at that time.

He was on edge and flighty, he was angry, telling the staff off, yelling. Horrid. But most of all I noticed how frightened he was, he said that he was running for his life. He was taking a heavier drug that changed his personality. He said that the dealers were after him and wanted him dead. The loss of his uncle, and the grief he was going through, was more than he could bear.

While still in the clinic Brett rang his sister, he didn't want me to be involved. He told my brother that his sister would help him, she would know what to do. Unfortunately, she was going through some of her own struggles at that time. Things between them got heated, and they had a fallout. Little did she know then that this would have a devastating effect on her later, more than she could bear.

Brett kept in touch with me and then came up to Newcastle to stay with me for a bit which turned into three months. It was lovely having him home, but I could see that he wasn't the same person I once spent a lot of time with. He was irritable this time and had a lot of fear in him. Something was going on.

While staying with me Brett did his first aid certificate so he could reapply for a job in security. He bought a light blue denim jacket on Layby. He loved that jacket (he wore this the day he disappeared). He had his eyes tested and got new glasses. He couldn't sit still so he was out and about every day, mainly up to the shops.

One day he felt it time to go home and face the music, whatever that was, I believe he was having a lot of problems in Orange with the drug dealers. I said to him, 'you came up here to get away because you were frightened. If you go back, what will you do, lock yourself in your unit?' I said, 'Why not stay here where you have the freedom to go where you want, no one knows you, you can get on a bus or train and go wherever you like'. So he changed his mind and stayed. I'm so glad he did!

Brett went back to Orange in April. I didn't hear much from him after that, I would just text and ask how he was. If he answered, he answered, if he didn't – it didn't matter. I knew he wasn't in a good place. Little did I know that 2021 would be my worst nightmare.

The beautiful blessing about this year was the birth of my great-granddaughter, born after Brett went back to Orange. She had a tough start, but she pushed through. Many prayers went up to God for this precious gem. She became the source of strength to get us through what was to come the following year. She was the bond that pulled us together. We are all so richly blessed! Brett didn't get to meet her, but I did send him photos with no replies.

Brett finally made contact with me again after his return to Orange in April. On 30December 2020, I was at the hairdresser and when I finished, I found six missed calls from Brett and messages saying 'Where are you? Ring me,' they were panic stricken. When I rang him, he said 'Mum, Mum I've done a terrible thing, I'm evil.' Oh, dear I thought. He then told me there had been an intimate moment between him and some girl he was with, and he felt so ashamed. I told him to hang in there and I'd call him back when I got home. He was so frantic, his thoughts were all over the place. My heart aches as I write this.

There was a friendship going on between him and this girl that Brett had known for many years. There seemed to be a lot of anxiety and stress going on in this friendship at the time. Brett did not trust the partner of this lady and had a fear that he was going to hurt her children. Brett felt desperate to stop him.

When I think about that call and play it back over in my mind, I can hear how deeply distressed he was over protecting these kids. He told me that if he didn't try and do something to protect them and something happened to them he wouldn't be able to live with himself. He had a very strong need to protect these children to keep them and their mother safe. It was crazy! He was filled with so much fear.

There was so much going on in his head at that time and it was crazy and stressful, not just for him but for me also. I tried so hard to talk him through all this stuff and to encourage him not to do anything that he would regret later. Brett was later arrested and charged with breaking and entering into this lady's house to hurt/warn this man not to hurt the children. He had on him some bi-carb soda and a hammer. The one thing that I'd tried to warn him about had happened. My brother Jack had also tried to talk to him about this very same thing but to no avail. We did our best and that's where we left it. We could do no more. I prayed.

He rang me just prior to his disappearance and talked about how he spent years blaming everyone else for his troubles, all the wrong that he had done and realised in the end that it was about him not other people. He couldn't understand how he could become such a monster and how evil he was. He hung up and then called back later to say 'I need help, I'm insane Mum, my brain is fried. I think there's more wrong with me than just bipolar.'

He felt that he needed to be reassessed and stated that no one would listen to his side of the story. All he wanted was to be loved, to be understood, and to be forgiven for the wrong he had done to others and to forgive those who wronged him. Most of all he wanted to forgive his father and his brother and sister. He wanted his family back.

On the 3rd of January '21 he rang me filled with fear and in tears asking me to pray for him, he said he needed to come back to God and trust Him. As I prayed for him he started to mingle his own prayer in with mine crying. This was late at night. This call was the most intense call I have ever had with Brett, it was I believe 'spiritual warfare.' This boy wanted redemption for all he had done wrong in his life. He wanted Jesus to save him and I believe he was.

He was also crying out for protection, I believe something was happening at the time that frightened him. Although I didn't know all that was going on inside him, I did witness the anxiety and pain in him and around him. I may not have him with me now, but I do believe I will see him again. I live in the blessed hope of Christ's soon return when we can be reunited together never to be separated again.

> *And God will wipe away every tear from their eyes; there shall be no more death, nor sorrow, nor crying. There shall be no more pain, for the former things have passed away.' Then He who sat on the throne said, 'Behold, I make all things new.' Revelation 21:4, 5.*

Brett always said he needed to be reassessed. He felt he had more than bipolar. 'There is something else wrong with me' he would say. He never felt safe within the mental health system, he was frustrated that no one would listen to his side of the story, not them nor his family.

Then I told him about a course I had done in mental health years prior. Brett had already been diagnosed with bipolar when I attended a course run by Mental Health. I wanted to try and understand more about him and how to take care of him in the right way. What I had discovered after a discussion with the mental health nurse, was that he was more schizoaffective bipolar than just bipolar.

When I told Brett, it resonated with him, he said, 'That's it, Mum, I knew there was something more wrong with me.' It was like a light had come on in his head and he was satisfied with the 'new diagnoses,' so to speak.

After Brett's disappearance I discussed this with the mental health worker at Bloomfield Mental Health Clinic in Orange and she agreed. She was going to put a team together and discuss strategies for how they could work with him when he came back home. Unfortunately, that never happened, a bit too late than I thought. This discussion should have taken place years before.

Brett stated at the end of 2020 that this breakdown was the worst that he'd ever been through, and that he would never recover from this. This was Brett's fourth major breakdown. He never recovered after his discharge from the mental health clinic. He also stated that he needed a mediator regarding his financial responsibilities and his care. Brett asked 'Mum, can you ring Helen, she'll come and help me.' Helen is a friend of mine who is a mental health worker in Newcastle.

I rang Helen and discussed the case with her, and she told me that Brett had needed to be in full-time care for a while and that he'd been a very sick man for a long time. She said her job is to place people with drug addictions and mental health disorders into group homes or rehabilitation centres.

She would assess him and get him into a group home in Newcastle where he would have the structure and routine, medication management and personal hygiene prompts that he needed. Also to be closer to his family, his sister and me. There were more facilities able to cater for his needs in Newcastle than in Orange. Arrangements were made by a friend to take me to Orange on Monday 4 January 2021 to pick Brett up as I don't drive.

Just before leaving for Orange, I received an unclear message from Brett, saying he had a counselling appointment at 11am on 4 January before he'd leave for Newcastle. Immediately below that he said, 'don't worry about it, all good, the counsellor's going to take me to the station on Wednesday and I'll get the train'.

There was a message missing between those two messages that I didn't understand. I was confused and tried to text and phone him, but he was not responding to me. Little did I know that this was the morning he was arrested by the police. I wasn't sure what to do so I rang Helen. She said, 'Just travel safe, all will work out.' She was basically saying 'Go in faith.'

We headed out the next morning at 10:30am on 4 January, 2021. We arrived at Brett's place at 2.30 pm, only to be told by him that he couldn't come because he had an appointment on Tuesday with another counsellor. As I walked around the unit, I was speechless, to call it a mess is an understatement, I've never seen his place in such a state. He always kept it reasonably clean. He had lost all ability to care for his unit let alone himself. I had some lovely times with Brett in this unit.

Brett made the decision not to come with us this time, he would come up on the train on Wednesday. So, we packed the car with the things he wanted to bring with him, and we left for Newcastle without him. We were just on the outskirts of entering Bathurst when Brett rang and said, 'I guess I've missed my ride' and said his Tuesday appointment had been cancelled (and by the way, there was no appointment) and he didn't want to stay in Orange. That didn't seem odd to me at the time, but it does now.

We turned around and went back to Orange to pick him up. I said to him 'have your bag packed and be ready to go when we get there'. It was a long tiring trip. We arrived back in Newcastle at my place at 11.10pm.

After a while that evening, Brett discovered that he didn't have his wallet and phone charger with him. We searched all his things but couldn't find anything. He seemed to become anxious. I tried to reassure him that everything would be okay and that I would get a phone charger and sort his cards out in the morning. It had been a long day, and we were both tired. I got him to have a shower and settled for bed. Not long after I went to bed, he came into my room, switched on the light and startled me.

I jumped and said, 'oh that light is bright Brett.'

He turned it off and left saying 'sorry, sorry, sorry Mum.'

I asked him if he was okay, and he said 'yes'. I didn't know then that that would be the last time I would hear his voice. I wished I'd gotten up and seen for myself that he was ok, but I was so tired from the trip back from Orange that I rolled over and went back into a deep sleep. In the end I do know this, he simply couldn't do life anymore.

Tuesday 5 January 2021. The next morning, I got up to go to the bathroom at 4.00am. Everything looked fine, his bedroom door was shut. I got up again at 6.00am and found both the front and back doors open and unlocked. There was paper on the floor at the back door with no writing on it. Then I found my torch and a small utility knife outside on the lid of the yellow bin. Down in the backyard I found Brett's rug rolled up in a ball near the hedge. I couldn't understand all of this, it made no sense to me.

I went to Brett's room and found him gone. On the floor there was paper, some screwed up and some not. Some had been sliced. Nothing had been written on them. I wondered if he wanted to say something and didn't have the words. That I will never know. I also found missing from the bedside table his keys, a bottle of water and his phone. I found his mobile phone under the bed several weeks later which the police had to take for their investigations. I then went to the kitchen and found my thermos mug missing and the coffee sitting on the kitchen bench. I thought 'okay, he's made himself a mug of coffee so he'll be back. He's just gone for a walk.'

The side gate I found was also unlatched which it never is. I'm very conscious of keeping that gate shut at all times. I kept a vigil six times a day at the front door watching and waiting, sobbing for Brett to walk up the street, and praying to God. And nothing. I then remembered my big Stanley knife on the shelf in the shed and thought 'no, no, no, not my knife.' I ran out and found it was gone too. My heart stopped with fear. Had he decided to commit suicide? I was beside myself.

I called the police, and they came out. I went through the procedure with them of all that had happened the night before and that morning. By Wednesday, Brett had been declared a missing person. I was shattered. I talked to God this whole time pleading for Him to bring him back. I kept saying, 'How can this be.' My other two children were struggling with grief in their own way.

I remember standing at the front door with my head resting on the screen sobbing watching for Brett to walk up the road. I did that six times a day for some time before I realised that I wasn't doing that as much. The whole time I talked with God. One day I realised that Brett wasn't coming back, it was a gut instinct.

One day I yelled at God and said, 'Why did you take my gentle giant from me? Then with tears I said to God, 'If you have allowed my Brett to be laid to rest, I ask for only one thing, that You give me the strength to endure, I cannot bear this alone.' Not only did He give me the strength, but He comforted me and gave me His [God] peace that only He can give that surpasses all understanding. Brett was in a bad place with his mental health. The torment and anguish I saw him go through was heart-wrenching.

Two weeks later I did make the trip back to Orange. I needed to search for myself as to where his wallet had gone. I found spare keys in Brett's things and thought, good I can get in. I informed the police of my decision; they were good with that and said that I was the only one who could do this. They asked me to let them know if I found anything. This time I went back with the same friend and his wife. Jack met us at the unit. The keys I found didn't fit so we had to find another way in. We found the kitchen window closed but not latched so Jack climbed in and let us in the back door. It's a wonder the neighbours didn't call the police, five people weren't exactly hard to see walking around someone's house.

I went straight to the lounge room; I went straight to the lounge, lifted the blanket up and there was his wallet. The phone charger was still plugged into the power board, why? Why did he suddenly change his mind to want to leave then and not on Wednesday? He wouldn't have left his phone and charger behind. I know he was filled with a lot of fear.

There are many questions unanswered, questions I can't answer, and I choose to leave these in God's hands. I cannot change what I cannot change, only what I can. We packed up Brett's music gear, I needed his files with whatever paperwork that was in them and the rest of the things I thought were important we packed in the car and headed back to Newcastle. What a relief it was to find the wallet! I phoned the Newcastle police and told them the good news. I tried to apply for a guardianship trustee to manage Brett's finances.

As part of the guardianship trustee application process, it needed a copy of his medical and psychiatric history. Because of his missing person's status many of the questions on the guardianship trustee application couldn't be answered as all we could write was 'missing' so we were required to put the detective's name on the application. As a result of this, the detective needed a copy of Brett's medical history.

After all that, I was then told that because Brett was a missing person. The guardianship board couldn't take on his case and that it would have to go to the Supreme Court. Seriously, it was one thing after another! I got legal aid to help with getting power of attorney so I could take care of closing Brett's accounts. This went on for weeks only to have the solicitors say, 'we've decided to wait until the Coroner makes his decision.' That can take years, I thought!

Twenty-nine days passed, from fifth of January to second of February 2021. No sign of my Brett whatsoever. Not seen nor heard from. His bank account has still not been touched. The case was turned over to the detective from Belmont police on 26 January 2021. It was here when I started writing my statement, not something I would wish upon my worst enemy. I could not describe what I was feeling. It's been a hard journey for my family and myself, and it continues. And not to mention grieving the loss of our brother as well.

I never went through this trauma alone, the detective asked if I would like to speak to a counsellor, and I agreed. This came through the missing persons group. A wonderful lady named Shantel called me and we began my journey together. Our meetings were via phone consult as it was through COVID lockdown. Our calls were a mix of pain, frustration, anger, regrets, even laughter. They were deep and meaningful, lifting every stone.

What a wonderful journey Jayne took me on. The bond between us was strong. When it was time for her to move on to another area, I cried. It was like she was leaving me even though I knew that her timing was right. During that time, I talked about my childhood and everything in between. So, she learnt of my Aboriginal background. It wasn't until she left and sent me the most heartwarming card telling me that she too was of the same background. She is the most loving, selfless, caring, compassionate person I have ever known. When I read and reread her card I said to God, 'There is no one who can take her place.'

I chose not to have another counsellor. I thought it impossible for someone else to carry on with my journey of grief. She was second to none and no one could fill that gap' so I thought, until I joined HammondCare in 2023. It was here I was offered pastoral care, I accepted straight away. And the healing sessions began again with Wendy. Another loving, selfless, wonderful, caring, compassionate person I thought I could never meet again. God is good! What I was saying I didn't need and what God was saying I did need are two different things.

In March 2021 I decided to make the trip back to Orange. My daughter drove me down and she would come back and pick me up when I was finished. I stayed for two weeks with my brother and his wife. My brother and I had to clean out Brett's unit, keep what was necessary and the rest we took to the tip. On our first day (Monday), I tripped in the garage and sprained my ankle ending up with a moon boot and crutches.

> *'For My thoughts are not your thoughts, nor are your ways My ways,' says the Lord.*
>
> *'For as the heavens are higher than the earth, so are My ways higher than your ways, and My thoughts than your thoughts. Isaiah 55:8, 9.*

I couldn't go with Jack on Tuesday, I needed to rest my ankle. We only had a week. Luckily, we had our nephew Luke come and help with all the dumping, and he cut all the long grass down or should I say weeds, they were four feet tall. I rang Housing to let them know that I was down to clear out the unit and hand the keys back. Sam, his name, was a lovely man, asked if we needed any help, then asked what my brother was using to take stuff to the tip. I said he had a trailer, so Sam sent out a skip bin. Housing was so good to us. And the cleaning and sorting began.

My sister Maddy came on Thursday, we got the rest of the cleaning done. Maddy was meeting up with her friends for afternoon tea so we both spent the afternoon with good company over a cuppa. Was a wonderful way to end that horrid day.

Jack then had to hand in and sign over Brett's unit keys to the Department of Housing the next day (Friday). My brother and I felt like we had thrown Brett out in the tip along with all his belongings. It was devastating.

Three weeks later after all of this and just before COVID-19, masks and lockdown set in, I started having heart palpitations in the middle of the night.

I was feeling really unwell. I rang GP Access and they sent a car out and I was taken to the hospital casualty dept where I was diagnosed with Afib.

Four times through that year I was put on a heart monitor at the hospital, only in casualty for about six hours each time. I was placed on heart medication by the cardiologist. And life goes on.

It's been a tough three years and ten months, but God has been good, faithful, and loving. His strength and peace have been given in abundance.

I also now have a care package with HammondCare and get help with the housework. I also have a volunteer support person just for that added help. A real blessing.

Brett's case is a cold case, even though he's missing they can't close it. The police are not actively looking for him but if any evidence comes up and sometimes it does, 20, 30, 40 years down the track, horrid thought, then the case is reopened. Especially if forensic finds that it was foul play. Most of the time, the perpetrators are dead anyway.

Even if this doesn't happen, justice will be served because God is a just God and he will avenge His children, those who have been mistreated and it will come out in the end. Families struggle to move forward because they have no answers. Not knowing is a difficult thing to go through.

This is a very special entry into the impact Brett made on one young boy who used to live next door to him in Orange. Jayden texted me one day in 2022 saying, 'has Brett been found?' I didn't know the name, so I asked who he was. And he came back with this text. He was 17 when he wrote this…

Brett was like an uncle to me, growing up as a kid he was the one to give me life advice when I needed it.I actually sat down with him the week before he left, and he was telling me how he'd been struggling lately, and then the next day he came back, and he was okay. I've honestly been lost without him. I'm glad I have memories of him. He is forever in my heart, not a day goes by that I don't think about him. I couldn't imagine the pain you and your kids must endure day by day.

What a treasure! Brett often sat and talked to young ones at the food pantry where he volunteered. He had a desire to help those who were struggling with mental health, to go through life like he was. He also chose not to have children for the same reason. The only thing he truly longed for was peace in his life and to be happy with his family.

It is now 2024 and it has been three years and 10 months since he walked out of my house and has never been found. His bank account remains untouched. Although we are broken by this tragedy we are starting to find peace. Only God knows where he is and what happened to him. In faith, I leave him in God's hands.

2010 - A Significant Year

Bus Accident

While working in the group homes, one day in 2010 I went to work as usual. The morning staff had taken the kids to their various day activities. In Condon Avenue nearby there was an activity centre that catered for the kids. One of the girls had been dropped off there and one near Marketown in Newcastle. I came in for the afternoon shift and headed off to pick up the first girl in the Toyota Hiace. It was wet and miserable.

I took my usual route but for some reason I crossed over to the right lane instead of staying in the left lane. When I got to the top of the hill before the Elermore Vale lights I could see a car coming up quickly on my left and she side-swiped and hit my front fender. I gripped the steering wheel tightly and went through the lights and pulled up outside the retirement village. I had Lois, a client, onboard and as we pulled up, I said to her 'are you ok? Did you hear that big bang?' I laughed, and she said 'yeah!' and laughed. I knew I needed to keep her calm as she had schizophrenia and could get quite upset very quickly. The lady who hit me was very upset and came up to me and I said 'what on earth were you doing, did you not see this is a disability bus?'

She was upset, it was raining so I invited her into the bus. She explained what had happened, that other cars in front of her had stopped suddenly, she'd hit the brakes and because of the water on the road she had lost control and skidded into the bus.

I said to her 'I am so sorry.' I told her who I was and that I was doing a client pick-up. I didn't have the work phone with me, so I went into one of the units in the retirement village where I pulled over. I knocked on one of the doors and told the lady my situation and asked if I could use her phone to ring my workplace.

The police came, took all the particulars and asked me if I could still drive, and he walked beside the bus until I got around the corner where we would be safe. We had to wait a few hours before work came to the rescue and the tow truck to get the bus.

Doris started to get a bit edgy but I managed to keep her occupied. Eventually, we were picked up and taken back to the group home. I hurt my back, and hands, being arthritic, never the same after gripping that wheel. I went on WorkCover. I was off for a couple of months then went back to work on light duties and was still having a lot of trouble.

I was living in Rutherford at that time. While I was off on compo, I slipped in the shower one night, I put my hand down to stop the fall and broke my wrist.

Brett was staying with me for a bit then and not well. I thought 'oh dear, I can't have him coming in to help me up because I'm naked!' So, I managed to get to my feet in agony, flick the water off and do what I could to dry myself. I got some clothes on using one hand and said to Brett, 'I've had a fall, I think I've broken my arm, can you help me?' He was a bit annoyed and wouldn't make any phone calls.

I managed to get myself together and called some friends who came and picked me up and took me to Maitland hospital. I was off on WorkCover at the time and now with a broken wrist, I had a cast for six or eight weeks and couldn't do anything. I am left-handed and had to learn very quickly how to use my right hand. I rang work and told them what had happened and they said, 'oh Lyn, you are in the wars!' I said, 'yeah and of all places to fall and break my wrist at home and not at work.' So, I still got nothing out of it.

I finally got back to work, due to the arthritis in my hands I started to have trouble with completing the activities of daily living caring for the clients such as putting on their shoes and socks. It was difficult because they have stiff joints and they don't really help, you've got to do all the pushing and prodding with tight socks that you can barely get on. My hands were starting to suffer. I had a health issue that needed major surgery and three days in hospital. During my time in the hospital, as I lay thinking about everything, I realised I couldn't go back to work.

'I'm done' I thought. Two of the registered nurses from the group home came and visited me there and one said, 'Tell me when you are going home and I'll come back and get you and take you home.'

I said to her, 'I may not come back to work.' She said to think about it. While I was at home, I rang her and asked if she would come and see me so she came out for a visit.

I had my resignation ready, and she said, 'I knew you'd do that; I didn't think you'd come back.'

I said, 'I can't do it anymore.'

Retirement 2010

I had a wonderful occupational therapist who made me soft and hard braces for my hands. She'd helped me set up my unit with disability aids, grab rails etc and anything else I needed. She told me I could get a disability pension and I said I'd been told that with only arthritic hands I wouldn't be eligible. She felt confident that I would. They don't allow it now but back then it was possible.

I had to see the doctor and then go to CRS, the rehab services in Maitland and I prayed about it. It was a stressful time. I said to God, 'I'm just going to leave it in Your hands, and You choose the people to have in my path.'

When I went in to have my interview I met a lovely lady, she was so great. I told her my story, all the problems I'd been having that year, the broken wrist, the bus accident and the surgery. She asked me about my work and what I'd done over the years, my work history.

She just said to me 'You have done your time Lyn, it's your time now to rest.' She told me that she doesn't make the decisions, Centrelink does but it depended on how she worded the letter. She told me to leave it with her. She also told me that with Centrelink there will be a gap between leaving work and getting the pension and there will be a payment like the dole, but I didn't have to look for work. It was a bridging payment between leaving work and getting the pension.

When it finally came through, I never had the bridge, I went from work straight to the disability pension. I praised and thanked God for His timing, He is so good. He just opened the doors, removed all obstacles and put me straight on the pension. It was so good and I got it fairly quickly. So that's where retirement started, I was 55 at the time. Now I didn't have to work and could rest and take care of myself. Hallelujah!

My Life Changes Direction

During that same year in 2010 I visited my younger sister Maddy in Narromine where she was living out on a property. During my stay we were driving out of town back to the property when Maddy pointed out a lane that Melinda lived in. Melinda was a lady that I grew up with in Orange and we went to the Adventist church when we were kids with another friend Helen.

I said 'oh that's great, ring her up, we'll go and visit, I haven't seen Melinda in years. We got to Maddy's place and arrangements were made to go and visit with her.

We went to visit Melinda that afternoon and she started talking about our friend Helen who I hadn't seen since the Cooranbong days. I was now living in Rutherford and in addition to my time in Queensland, it would have been 10-15 years since I'd been in contact with Helen.

Melinda started telling me how Helen had become very sick and nearly died three times and had been anointed each time. I was shocked, I said, 'I must go and visit her when I get home.' I recall having her number at home somewhere. We had a lovely visit with Melinda and after my stay with Maddy ended, I headed home.

As I was driving back to Rutherford on the way home the radio became staticky, and I didn't want the silence. I had some cassettes in the glove box, so I reached over, fumbling. I pulled out a tape. It was Daniel O'Donnell's Inspirational's. I thought 'that'll do' and stuck it in the tape deck. These were all the old hymns that I loved. *The Old Rugged Cross, Softly and Tenderly Jesus is Calling.* All these beautiful old hymns that I grew up with and loved, absolutely loved as a kid.

As I got through Denman I could see the bridge, I knew the turn-off to Newcastle was just past the bridge. I was thinking 'great, the last stretch, before the turn off to Newcastle, I'm not far from home.' I was tired. This is going through my mind, but the music is still playing. As I crossed the bridge, I was in deep thought listening to the words of the songs playing, I became emotional. I lost all recollection of what was going on around me. I just drove. I was so engrossed in the music I was crying.

When I came back from wherever I was hanging out in my head, there was a big green sign that read, 'Welcome to Muswellbrook.' I thought 'You've gotta be kidding me, how'd I get here? Muswellbrook!'

I missed the sign saying Newcastle. I noticed that I'd passed a truck route which bypassed Muswellbrook. I thought 'I can't go all the way back because I don't know how far I've travelled; I'll take the truck route.'

So, I turned around and took the bypass. Which still brought me back out on the New England highway, and I saw a sign that said Singleton 38km. I said, 'you have got to be kidding me!' When you take the Newcastle turn, you miss Singleton and come out just before Branxton and then it's Lochinvar and Rutherford (home). That's how far out I was. I did find out later that I actually drove 27k out of my way with no recollection of that trip. What a journey!

So, I just said 'well Lord I have no idea why I've come this way. But you know.' I call it my time with God.

I finally got home and found the address book. I hoped Helen's number was still the same. I rang her a couple of days later and said to her, 'I'm sorry it's been so long since I last spoke to you.' I told her where I had been and that I'd had the opportunity to visit Melinda who told me that she had been really sick, that she nearly died. 'I know it's been a lot of years,' I said.

She said, 'I have been very sick, I was anointed three times. I said, 'Helen this is terrible, we've got to meet up'. She said, 'sounds good to me, do you want to come out tonight?' I said, 'look I've just got home from work and I'm really tired.' 'Not a problem' she said, 'just come out when you're ready.'

I went to my room to change, and had a strong impression that said, 'ring Helen and go.' So, I rang her back and said 'Helen, I'm coming out.'

She said, 'oh ok, no worries'.

I showered, changed and drove from Rutherford to Windemere Park. We had a wonderful time reminiscing, chatting, and laughing. It was fabulous. Helen then looked at her watch and said, 'I've got to go, I have a women's prayer meeting on a Wednesday night, you're welcome to come with me.'

I just said, 'I'm not interested in that sort of thing.' I'd been out of the church for quite a while since my mid-30s, I just went my own way.

She said 'I can feed you and you can come with me' but I declined. So, we had to wind up and say goodbye. I hadn't seen her for such a long time. Anyway, unexpectedly, I just said 'I think I will come with you.' I had no interest, yet the pull to go was so strong. God's plan was in place.

The ladies were sitting around in a circle, about nine of them and I was introduced to each one. They were reading a little book; a devotional and I said 'what are you reading? It was so beautiful, I said, 'I want one of those books!'

I was so engrossed in hearing these devotionals. Of all names, the book was called *Jesus Calling* and this is what these devotionals were doing, calling me back to Christ. I was almost bouncing off the seat, I wanted this book!

The lady who owned the house said, 'I only bought enough for us girls, I don't have any more left.' I said, 'that doesn't matter, where did you get it from?' I was just so desperate for these words. Anyway, at nine o'clock it was time to go. We all got up to leave, the lady who lived in the house was at the door.

As I approached her, she said, 'Lyn when we finished up, I was impressed to go into my room and open the bottom drawer of my dresser and found one last book.' She said, 'I distinctly remember that I had no more, this book has your name on it.' And she gave it to me. I couldn't believe it. A God moment I call it.

I went home and pored over this book every day and I cried every day. That's how empty I felt. That's where my space was, empty. I was alone. I'd had a work accident, I'd been in hospital for surgery, and all the stuff I had to go through getting the disability pension, I felt lost. This book was filling the void, and I said, 'I want what this book is offering me.' So, I started to visit Helen often and we started to hang around together. She invited me to Hillview Adventist Church which she attended at the time. She then started attending the Memorial Church on Freemans Drive.

One day when I was still working, Helen rang me and said there's a seminar happening in Newcastle called the All Power Health Seminar run by Leo Schreven. I said, 'that name rings a bell, I've seen it advertised on the TV.'

She said, 'would you like to go?' and I said, 'yeah why not, I'll go.' I was working at the time at the group homes. I wasn't sure I'd be able to attend the seminar as I did weekend shifts at the homes. I did go though and found it very interesting and quite enjoyed it. I attended all the programs.

All Power 2 was Leo's next program, called Revelation Seminar. That was the theology side, and it was held at Hamilton church. It was the same situation; I had to get time off work. I would get home, shower, dress and drive to Hamilton for the seminar. Leo gave the introduction of the seminar and started to talk about the book of Revelation. As I sat there I thought 'hang on a minute, I know this stuff.' I learned this as a kid. It was like something just clicked inside of me and I couldn't get enough.

After the seminar finished, I walked out and there was a table in the foyer with books on it, so I asked the man standing there, 'what can I read?

The man was Pastor Mike Robertson who gave me a book called *The Story of Redemption*.

While I was there, Pastor Justin Lawman and Helen were at the other table. Helen was looking at all the books on the display table. Justin says to Tina, the receptionist, while pointing to me 'get that lady's name, address and phone number.'

Helen turned and saw me and said to him, 'you want her details, do you? I know her, I brought her to these seminars. That's where it all started. Pastor Mike eventually came out to Rutherford and had bible study with me. I call it God at work behind the scenes.

Leo was in Australia, and he was coming to do a seminar at Armidale and Tina asked me if I would go. I said I didn't know if I could make it and she said, 'We'll just see what God says.' And I just said 'Yeah, right, and laughed.' Anyway, I then had the bus accident, and I went back to Memorial Church and told Tina 'You wouldn't believe what happened, I've had a bus accident and I'm off work for two months.'

She said, 'God is good!' and smiled at me.

I ended up in Armidale at the seminar and I was working on the door, greeting people.

I was baptised on 20 June 2010, age 55. That was the third time. The first two were at ages 13 and 21. I wanted Leo to baptise me, he said he would be delighted.

He said, 'I would travel back to Australia just to baptise you without a seminar.' Leo came back for his last seminar that was to run at Wyee Church.

Tina arranged my baptism. Helen made all the baptismal cards, and I was baptised Sunday morning at Memorial Church with the seminar held that afternoon at Wyee.

My daughter Jayne and granddaughter were there. A pastor from Wyee church attended with Leo, Pr Vadim Butov who did the sermonette, Pr Justin Lawman, and Pr

Mike Robertson.

I was blessed to have all five evangelists attend my baptism which is rare I'm told. It was an amazing day. This time round I made the decision to go back to God, not the church as I had done in the past. Best decision I ever made!

Volunteer Work

As I write this I have been working as a volunteer for about ten years. I volunteered at the ADRA Op shop in Cessnock for four years. As we had our own pantry, we often fed people when they came into the shops wanting food or needing clothing, especially the children. We also supplied furniture for those who had none, whatever their need. We did our best to supply.

I then worked with Booragul SDA church food pantry with the Samoans for five and a half years on reception. I enjoyed the Samoan people. They were loving, kind and great to be around.

Up until recently I was with Hamilton SDA church Food Pantry and volunteered there for over two years on the service desk. I loved my work as a volunteer. It was the joy of giving my time to serve others. I enjoyed that. I have now retired from that as well. What will I do next?

Guidance from God

I read two books that helped me greatly when I lived in Boolaroo, I was 40 at the time. The first was, *The Strong-Willed Child* by Dr James Dobson. And the second was *ADD in Adults*, by Dr Gordon Serfontein.

Strong-willed children need to be treated differently, disciplined differently to what you do with others. What you do with the others might work for them but may not necessarily work for a strong-willed child. So you need to change the method and do it differently.

I was probably an ADHD child also. I think Mum was frustrated, she didn't know what to do. The book *ADD in Adults* was given to me by a friend. I read that and it was fascinating. It was like all the pieces of the puzzle of my life fell out of the sky and fell into place. Everything that was missing came together. I said to this friend of mine 'you knew, didn't you?'

She said, 'yeah I did.'

I said, 'why didn't you tell me?'

She said, 'it was better for you to read about it and discover it yourself. You wouldn't have listened to me.'

I wished I'd had these books earlier in my life.

Personal Interactions

I love to talk to people in supermarkets. One day an elderly lady came up to me and said, 'do you work here?' and I said 'no, I'm just looking for something'. She said 'I'm going to ask you a question because you look like you know exactly what you're doing'.

That made me chuckle. I asked her what she was looking for and she told me and I said 'if you go for this, it's the best brand. This is what I use, it might be a little bit dearer, but you won't get the nasties in it', so she took it.

When we got to the checkout, the elderly lady went through before me and waved, said 'thank you for the chat'.

I said, 'yeah, thank you it was great'.

Then I put my groceries through the checkout, and I noticed the lady coming back and I said, 'did you leave something behind?'

'No', she said, 'I was just so thrilled with our conversation that I had to come back to thank you again.'

I said 'I'm just glad I was able to help you.

A Divine Appointment on Forgiveness

I was walking up to the shops one day when I reached the crossroad lights. I met a lady waiting for the lights to change, she was heading to the shops as I was, we both said 'hello' and started chatting.

As the lights changed we walked together chatting along the way. I don't know how it came up, but she talked about the hatred and bitterness she had towards her brother. She couldn't trust him. She said, 'I will never, forgive him for what he did to me.'

This lady had been holding onto this bitterness for a long time. So, I shared with her the benefits of forgiveness. I said to her 'When you don't forgive someone, that anger stays in you, and the only person it will destroy is you. Your brother won't care, he's not even thinking about it.'

I said 'You're the one who's still suffering under his abuse. So, for you to heal and move forward is to rid yourself of the bitterness and to forgive him.'

She said 'Oh, I can't forgive …never.'

I said to her, 'forgiveness frees you from the bondage of resentment and retaliation. But while you hold onto your bitterness, he will continue to have full control even if you never see him again. That's the power of hatred toward another human. It doesn't excuse him for what he has done to you, he is still accountable for his actions, the charges are still there but they're just no longer on your shoulders. You give it back to him, and that releases you to move forward, and you will find a heavy weight will lift off your shoulders.

That's the power of forgiveness.'

She said she had never heard this before. We continued to chat until we reached our fork in the road where we parted at Hungry Jacks. Before she went her way and I went mine, she couldn't thank me enough for the chat.

I believe she had some of that weight removed from her shoulders that day. This lady lived in the block of units near the lights and I have never seen her since. I believe it was a divine appointment. She learnt something that day, and God willing she followed it through and is a much happier person.

The Gift of Forgiveness - Connecting Matters

'Forgiveness is the fragrance that the violet sheds on the heel that has crushed it.'
Mark Twain

Ephesians 4:32 : And be kind to one another, tender-hearted, forgiving one another, even as God in Christ forgave you.

A Devotional I read:

Yet I have learned that while I can't control the behaviours of others, I am responsible for my own behaviours, including the extension of forgiveness.

Whenever there is a lack of forgiveness, a wall goes up between the parties involved.

God calls us to forgive others so we can be forgiven.

Matthew 6:14,15: For if we forgive men their trespasses, your heavenly Father will also forgive you. But if you do not forgive men their trespasses, neither will your Father forgive your trespasses.

How We Treat Others

This story comes from a time in 2021 when we struggled to get toilet paper. I was at the bus stop when an elderly gent sitting and waiting looked up at me and started to talk. We chatted until our bus came in; he ushered me to hop on before him. I sat in my seat and as the man walked past, he stopped and proceeded to take two rolls of toilet paper out of a freezer bag and handed them to me saying, 'I'd like to give you these.'

I said, 'Oh no you keep them I have some at home.'

He said, Woollies were giving four out in a bag to the elderly for free.' He was persistent about me having them and I said, 'What have I done to deserve these?' and he said, 'You were kind to me.'

I thanked him and he went and sat in his seat. I could only think that maybe not many people speak to him, I have no idea, but what a gift it is to give! The blessings will always come rolling back two-fold. God loves a cheerful giver!

I was at a bus stop in Swansea sometime back after spending the day with my sister waiting for the bus to go home. An elderly gent walked past in his dirty torn garments, his long dirty hair and beard looking like he hadn't had a bath in a long time. He was smelling like a polecat in a strong wind coming straight at you, his odour was high. He began to speak to me and I responded.

As we talked back and forth the smell got a bit too much for my nostrils so I took two steps away from him, in that split second I said, 'Lord, that was the wrong thing to do' and

I took those two steps back toward him and we continued our conversation. The bus came in and we both boarded that bus, the bus then reeked of his odour. And I thought 'who cares!' Thank you, God, for the blessing.

Why do I tell you this? Who are we to condemn when we are no different than anyone else on this planet. The Bible says, in Isaiah 64:6, *But we are as an unclean thing, and all our righteousness, are as filthy rags .... we are all sinful creatures in need of a Saviour.*

Be kind to everyone peeps, regardless of their race, colour, looks and personality, whatever their garments may look like or smell like. God loves a cheerful giver/carer.

'Love means doing what God has commanded us, and He has commanded us to love one another.......'2 John1:6NLT.

To do that is to spend time with God in His word every day.

Today 23 September 2024

In April I had an echocardiogram done to check how my heart was doing. Every year on Brett's birthday, June 3, I go over to Warners Bay and walk along a special part of the walking path that juts out over the water, an Aboriginal memory walk, just beautiful to spend time doing that. This year it marked his 51st birthday. I wanted to get flowers but couldn't afford them this time.

My support person Rachel turned up to take me to a doctor's appointment and then over to Warners Bay. When she arrived, she had a small bunch of purple flowers and a box of chocolates. They were beautiful! I told her I didn't have any flowers this time for Brett, then watching Rachel as she put the flowers into the vase, I realised that it wasn't about Brett this time, it was my turn to receive flowers. I went to my appointment, then we drove to the lake at Warners Bay. As we walked along the path we read the poetry excerpts written on the railing together it was lovely. On our way back we did the same on the other side.

When we got back to the resting place where you can sit a spell we stopped and chatted for a while. When it was time to leave, we got up and started to walk. As I looked out over the water, I felt this amazing peace come over me and I said to Rachel, 'I just had a heavy burden lifted off my shoulders. God has healed me.'

I had peace. It was amazing! I knew that this was a God intervention, and He was with me. It was a powerful moment. I told Rachel later that we were standing 'In the presence of God.' She felt it too.

On June 6 I went back to the Cardiologist to get the results from my Echocardiogram, the Dr said my heart was good, heart rate was 49 which is normal. He stopped the one medication I wanted to be rid of because of its high toxicity and lowered the dosage of another from 75mg twice daily to 50mg twice daily. He was surprised that I was feeling so well. He then wanted me to wear a heart monitor for 24 hours to check my daily heart rate. Within a few days, I had the heavy burden of Brett lifted and filled with peace that only God can give and an excellent report from the cardiologist! The blessings were overflowing. In the one week I had my heavy burden lifted, my medications reviewed and changed for the better. I had been praying for healing and that one drug in particular would be stopped. Three and a half years after Brett's disappearance my prayers were answered! Praise God for His goodness.

On 18 July, I went back to the Cardiologist to get the results of the Holter monitor. The test was excellent, and my heart rate was normal, he was dumbfounded, and he asked me how I was feeling, and I said really well. There was nothing more he could ask; he just said you won't need to come back to see me unless there are changes. Great news. In 2021 I was diagnosed with AF and prescribed heart medication. Praise God!

I give God the glory for my life and where I am today.

Telling my Story

I look back over my life and see now the footprints of God and all His goodness falling like autumn leaves around me, and how He led and protected me. How I was loved by Him. Even if I had parents, I thought didn't love me, even when I felt different, even when I felt rejected, I know I had a God in heaven who loved me, and He took care of me. I give God the glory for all that He has done, is going to do, and I leave my future in His hand.

My life has been full of both good and bad experiences. I once learned about the 'filing cabinet' analogy. With all the traumas through your life, you picture yourself sitting on the floor and emptying all the memories, good or bad, and lay them out onto the floor. You then pick through and only put back what is good and useful. Anything that is upsetting or not useful, you dispose of it. You sometimes need to do this more than once, and at certain times throughout your life.

As the years have gone by, I feel I have moved from having a filing cabinet full of stuff I did not need. In my journey I have been able to shrink the harmful stuff down to a suitcase, then to a backpack, then a bumbag. I now feel after writing my story that I can let go of the last of these bad memories (bumbag gone) and keep only the ones that give me joy. I may have picked up some new difficult memories along the way and have been capable of letting them go. I feel lighter now and leave the garbage, when necessary, outside the fence for the garbage man to take away.

The most precious treasures of my life are my children, my grandchildren, and my great-granddaughter. I am richly blessed and to each one, I love with all my heart. There is never a moment that you don't cross my mind, I love being your Grandma. You are all beautiful, you are all special, you are all important and you are all unique. You are someone nobody can replace. And remember the God of the universe loves you all with an everlasting love that no one can separate you from.

2024: Brett's been gone three years, Tom's been gone four years, Jazz's been gone seven years. Life goes on, the pain does soften at some point and somewhere in the pain of my loss, I found peace. I miss them and hold them tenderly in my heart. And by God's grace, we heal.

Yea, though I walk through the valley of the shadow of death, I will fear no evil; for You are with me; Your rod and Your staff, they comfort me. Psalm 23:4

~ Prayer of Serenity ~

*God grant me the **Serenity***

To accept the things I cannot change,

***Courage** to change the things I can*

*and the **Wisdom** to know the*

difference

Until the Clouds Roll Back

Brett's song

Verse 1
A little baby born on the third of June,
Nineteen seventy-three, too fragile, too soon.
He struggled for breath, held on so tight,
Five long months, but he fought for life.
A brother named Jeff by his side each day,
Laughing and playing in simple ways.

Verse 2
Then Jayne came, a sister so dear,
Three little hearts full of laughter and cheer.
They made happy memories wherever they'd go,
Moments of joy only family knows.
Brett grew strong, playful and free,
A tender soul for all to see.

Chorus
Life had its ups, life had its downs,
But Brett fought bravely through it all.
A sensitive heart, so deep, so kind,
Carrying more than the eye could find.
Though the road was hard, his love remained,
Forever held, forever named.

Verse 3
At five and a half he walked through school doors,
An emotional child, feeling so much more.
As teenage years came, the shadows grew long,
Mental health battles, trying to stay strong.
Then family broke, the pieces all spread,
Children and parents with wounds left unsaid.

Verse 4
Illness came, and the weight was too much,
Yet still he showed that gentle soft touch.
Loved beyond words, though the pain ran deep,
Some hurts are heavy, too hard to keep.
At forty-seven he slipped from our sight,
Gone from this world into silent night.

Chorus
Life had its ups, life had its downs,
But Brett fought bravely through it all.
A beautiful soul, tender and true,
Loved by many, missed by a few.
Though the case is closed, our hearts still cry,
Memories live and never die.

Bridge
Each passing day a thought appears,
A song, a place, a wave of tears.
Grief walks slowly, healing takes time,
Every heart mourns in its own design.
No kiss can heal this aching pain,
But love remains, it still sustains.

Final Chorus
We look ahead to that glorious day,
When Jesus comes to lead us home.
No more crying, no more pain,
No more death, no sorrow's chain.
The former things will pass away,
All things new, forever stay.

Outro
Until that day, let love be strong,
Help each other carry on.
For broken hearts will one day see,
Eternal peace, perfect and free.
Until the clouds roll back in light,
We hold you close… till heaven's sight.

www.ingramcontent.com/pod-product-compliance
Lightning Source LLC
Chambersburg PA
CBHW042127100526
44587CB00026B/4195